THE POWER OF
LABELS

THE POWER OF LABELS

How do we get Labeled?
How do Labels predetermine our Lives?
How to get Rid of them and Live a happier Life...

Marsy Beron

authorHOUSE®

AuthorHouse™ UK Ltd.
1663 Liberty Drive
Bloomington, IN 47403 USA
www.authorhouse.co.uk
Phone: 0800.197.4150

Translated by Boryana Savova
Illustrations by Dimana Doykova

This book does not provide professional psychiatric or psychological counseling, advice or services. If you need therapy, professional consultation, or psychiatric consultation, we recommend you consult with a licensed mental health professional in your area. The exercises, information, and tips are for informational purposes only, and are in the nature of a self-help book rather than a treatment service.

Published by AuthorHouse   03/21/2014

ISBN: 978-1-4817-9846-4 (sc)
ISBN: 978-1-4817-9845-7 (hc)
ISBN: 978-1-4817-9847-1 (e)

Contents

Foreword

How this book was created

When I started to ponder on the subject of labels and their impact on people's confidence and behavior, I had no idea that one day my notes would turn into a book. This was some kind of personal therapy. The notes helped me go back to my diverse problems and give more in-depth consideration to the various aspects of the impact of labels on my present behaviour. I remembered painful moments from my childhood and my youth, I analyzed them, and realized that under the influence of others and their judgment and opinions of me I have strayed too much from the real "me", that my potential in many areas has remained underdeveloped, and I have turned into . . . or have remained?! . . . a scared, uncertain and painfully sensitive child, who doesn't fit into the world of adults.

„What would people say?" never really interested me much but rather people as a whole, society. It turned out that I was actually addicted to the approval of those, closest to me, who did not always approved of my actions, intentions, even my beliefs about life. This made me suffer, it disillusioned me, it made me procrastinate both with regard to my decisions and my actions—I was too afraid not to make another mistake and disappoint someone. At the time, I did not realize that what others perceived as a mistake was simply my own path. I achieved my goals slowly and with great effort, some of them I gave up halfway, others I didn't even start. Why was that? I even laugh now when I remember how for many years I considered patience one of my greatest assets. I managed to look at things from another angle, from another perspective, and what I saw was hesitation, procrastination, endless rethinking and analyses of the situation—all out of fear of making a mistake. At the same time, I underestimated my success as my internal criteria were higher than the conventional. So, I could not be happy for it, even though everybody praised me—inside my head I was far from perfection.

And so, musing over my dissatisfaction with myself, my life, and my reactions when communicating with others (often exaggerated or inadequate), I discovered the numerous labels which distorted my own perception of myself and stood in my way in even basic everyday situations.

From time to time, I would share with my few friends what I had discovered about myself, analyzing it, and . . . surprise-surprise!—It turned out that the problem was not just mine. They, too, had been through similar situations in their past, they too had been labeled, and this stood in their way. During our conversations, they started to make discoveries about themselves—about thoughts and actions they had failed to control consciously.

Labels and labeling turned out to be a widespread psychological phenomenon.

When I started my training to become a Gestalt* psychotherapist, this conviction of mine was further confirmed. Everybody had labels, but not everybody was aware of that fact. My colleagues and I were different people with different paths in life, but too often did it turn out that we had been through similar life experiences. The differences came from the response and perception aspects—some had been crushed under this burden, others had escaped almost unimpaired. And of course, the labels each one of us had given to themselves, played a major role in this.

During the training process, and later on in my work with clients, with the accumulation of examples and insights into the "labeling" phenomenon, the idea to turn my notes into a book took shape—I sincerely hope that many of you will find it useful.

---

* **Gestalt therapy** is an existential/experiential form of psychotherapy that emphasizes personal responsibility, and that focuses upon the individual's experience in the present moment, the therapist-client relationship, the environmental and social contexts of a person's life, and the self-regulating adjustments people make as a result of their overall situation. Gestalt therapy was developed by Fritz Perls, Laura Perls and Paul Goodman in the 1940s and 1950s

Some of the exercises which I have recommended come from my own battle with labels, the rest has been borrowed from the Gestalt psychotherapy. One of the main Gestalt principles is that mental phenomena awareness should go through bodily sensations. For example, when we suffer, we have to focus on the body and try to find out where the pain resides, in what area of the body we feel discomfort.

In my personal process I discovered that the "materialization" of the labels seems to render them powerless, it makes them visible and easier to remove. Such are "the weed in my garden", "the bricks or wooden blocks in my backpack" and the "mine field" exercises.

All physical actions we undertake in the "Label Removal" process will help us present them to our mind as material entities, which will enable us to remove them with greater ease. Because, how could we otherwise, overcome something elusive, without form and colour, something we cannot see or touch? The power of labels is like an invisible pressure coming from all directions, which intercepts our thoughts and actions, distorts beyond recognition the mirror, reflecting our body and soul, and makes us vulnerable to the pain of the past and the fear of the future.

Another major principle of Gestalt psychotherapy, which you may recognize in the exercises and explanations of the "Label Removal" process, is the "HERE and NOW" principle. Because, life is that, which happens at this moment, in this place, in this situation—we can build it up, or change it now. And the labels are the screeching break which prevents us from making the decisive step, or stops us dead in our tracks just as we aspire towards our goal. Perhaps it would be better to put the "breaks" into the neutral position and firmly move on—to a more unbiased self-esteem and confidence, rather based on our qualities than our flaws, don't you think?

Marsy Beron

Don't worry, you are not going to crash, our brains are well equipped with enough mechanisms to regulate the speed and avoid hazardous situations.

And so, have a pleasant journey!
I'll see you at the finish line which I have yet to reach myself . . .

From the Author

Introduction

How do we get Labeled?

Graphically, the process can be presented as follows:

Judgments=>labels=>beliefs=>personal qualities=>success/failure

When judgment is passed by the people who surround us, it is imprinted in our minds—the neurons in our brains do their work, establishing connections even when the tiniest of data is entered through our senses. If it is an isolated judgment, or is passed by a person outside our immediate circle, the trace it leaves is pale and weak and would not affect our overall behavior now, or in the future. But if it comes repeatedly from someone we are close to, and is confirmed by others as well, it would be deeply imprinted in our minds and would become a label. Whether a label would turn into a belief or not depends mostly on time—on how long we have been subjected to its influence—its emotional charge that affects us, and our resistance to it. Believe it or not, under the influence of labels attached to us, which have become a part of our idea of who we are, we form the qualities of our character, and they in turn, determine the success or failure of all our endeavors.

In the course of our interaction with others we may receive both positive and negative labels. Thus, the main graphic of the process can be presented as follows:

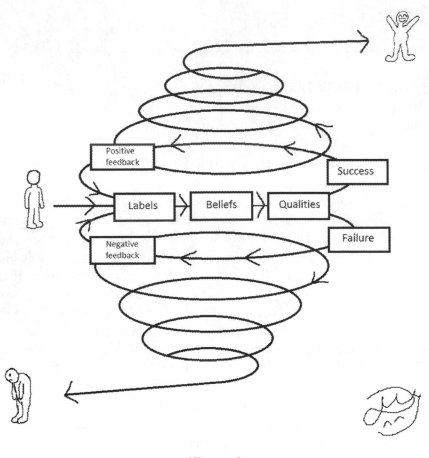

(*Figure 1*)

And here we go again—back to where we started—the beaten track—it feels like a vicious circle of which we cannot get out. It seems to me, this is rather a spiral that we enter and with every next round upwards or downwards, we affirm and consolidate the labels, beliefs and our qualities, and they, in turn, determine the outcome of our actions—success or failure.

And while we need not worry about the positive labels and qualities that get us closer to the success, we have to work on the negative ones, in order to break the vicious circle and get out of the spiral which pulls us downwards. If we manage to get rid of the negative labels, we will gradually form new beliefs and qualities, raise our self esteem, and thus, improve our chances of success altogether. Naturally, this cannot be achieved in a day or a week—the change requires effort and focused work on oneself.

Reversal of the Process—elimination of Labels

How long will the road to change be is strictly individual—the duration of the reverse process, however, depends on a number of factors, mostly on how long you have lived with your negative labels and to what extent they have become your beliefs and traits.

So, the reverse process requires conscious efforts on your part. But where do we begin? The removal of labels must go through several stages, the main ones being:

1. **Becoming aware of the labels.**

You will see that it's not that easy. There are labels we have carried since childhood that are so deeply rooted that we have accepted them as our traits, or flaws. Many of the labels we carry, we have given ourselves and then confirmed to the extent whereby we say "Well, that's who I am". And we believe it, shunning out any possibility of change. It is easier to recognize the labels which feel alien to us, although we have carried them for years—like other people's distorted ideas about us which we reject.

2. **Analyzing judgments which are the basis for the labels in our minds.**

Who gave them to us, in what circumstances did it happen, how important or close to us was the person who passed the judgment? Was this a one-off occasion, or did it happen many times? Was it one or several people who passed the judgment that turned into a label for us?

3. **Realizing the harm from the negative labels.**

Can you remember, how many times negative labels have blocked your way to success, been an obstacle in your relationships with intimate or business partners, how many times have you given up, achieving something important to you, believing that you do not have it in you, or that you are undeserving? Bad memories are a painful thing, yet if we do not recognize the reasons for what has happened and eliminate them, we risk constantly reproducing bad memories and discontent.

4. The decision to change.

There is a negative aspect of this process called procrastination. I am not talking about promises and decisions we have failed to follow up on, in order to overcome bad habits, unacceptable behavior and resolve problems, postponed for months and years. I am not talking about forced decisions either. The decision to change should reflect your own conscious desire. And you should not be bothered whether others like it or not, no matter how close they might be to you. Make up your mind and make the change for yourself.

5. Specific steps to remove labels.

The reasons for the appearance of our labels and the specific steps for their removal will be reviewed further down. Here is how the process can be presented graphically:

Intention to change ==>recognizing labels ==>removal of negative labels and their replacement with positive ones ==> their adoption to the point of becoming beliefs ==>quality formation==>success==>getting positive feedback/labels==>consolidation of positive labels==>consolidation of the new beliefs ==>consolidation of new qualities==> achieving new success.

And so on, until we enter the positive section of the graphic above (*Figure 1*). The first steps will be shaky and uncertain, and probably not too successful, but it is important for you not to give up. I can assure you, perseverance shall bear fruit, and they will taste sweet.

Everything begins in childhood

Hardly anyone would disagree with this statement. In childhood, the grounds are laid, upon which the new individual starts to build up his/her basic qualities, habits and attitudes. Unfortunately, it is then, that the main fears are instilled and complexes developed henceforth. The little person finds himself in an adult environment whereby everyone has the specific character and traits, as well as a different approach to him, very often based on different ideas of what is right or wrong way to raise a child. Since his/her first cry, the child is subjected to diverging influences on behalf of adults. Instinctively, he/she develops strategies to react to each adult in their environment. And while in the beginning the child is limited to the company of his/her parents, siblings, grandparents only, with each passing year, the circle of people with whom he/she interacts expands to involve his/her peers, the neighbours' kids, the kids of relatives, then his/her classmates, teachers, the teenage "pack", as well as the interesting representatives of the opposite sex.

When does childhood really end? With the coming of age? With the first sex? When we get drunk for the first time? With the wedding or when we become parents? There is no definitive answer. All of the above is the general belief which through the centuries human society has created to make things easier for itself—it classifies us as young, adults or old.

Childhood takes as long as it takes for each one of us. And even when it ends, we keep part of it which we carry with us for a long, long time, sometimes until the end. One of the things we also keep on a subconscious level from the earliest childhood is labels. They can be positive or negative, and sometimes they manifest in such unusual and varied ways that even an in-depth analysis of our behaviour and feelings can hardly reach the root cause, buried somewhere deep in our past—our childhood.

Out of the numerous factors that have an impact on us and create conditions for labeling, we shall review only the basic ones: parents, school, friends, etc.

Parents

In their strife to raise us well and protect us from trouble, our parents often harm us. In time, we do the same to our kids.

There is no school for parents, and as no one was born with a "how to" manual—we all learn as we go along. But do we always manage—as far as it is within our grasp—to build up good character, high self-esteem and a stable value system in our children? We exert influence on them in many ways, but since the subject of this book is the LABELS we attach unintentionally to them, or in efforts to teach them, let us review only them.

Imagine a ball of clay—the drier it gets, the harder it becomes to mould. We cannot afford to lose a moment if we want to shape it into a beautiful figurine—the nearest thing to our idea of a piece of art. The character of the young child is similar to that. The movements of our hands (in this case our words and gestures) should be very careful, in order to achieve the desired effect. Our absence from the educational process, whether for a short, or a longer period of time, no matter if it is a physical or psychological absence—affects the character of our children. A crack opens here, a twist happens there, some irregularities appear that we'd rather not allow to develop now, than try to fix later.

First Mistake

The effect we seek is not always congruent with what the child is naturally drawn towards.

If your child constantly rejects your advice, or insistence on a particular type of behaviour, think where you are making a mistake. Talk to your child and maybe you will find out the reasons for the rejection. Even if you don't find fault in yourself, you'd better change your tactics, instead of going the old way in the hope that one day you are going to break the child into accepting your point of view on a given issue. You don't think you are perfect, do you? Then, why do you want to produce your exact same replica in the face of your child?

Second Mistake

We expect that our kids will handle all mundane activities like adults.

Nagging of the type "you always break stuff when you wash the dishes" does not really help, just the opposite—it works against your desire to teach the child to help you with the chores at home. Next time the kid has to do the work instead of you, they will approach it with reluctance. It will not be because the child will remember what the broken glass or dish looked like, but the unpleasant feeling they had when you reproached them will sting them. Unintentionally, you have labeled them "clumsy".

It was a different story with me, but the suggestion was the same. In my early teenage years, when everybody strived to look great, I started to iron my own clothes. Well, it was then that I became famous for "you haven't burnt only what you haven't ironed." Not to mention the arguments about the forgotten plugged in iron. The result—more clothes that do not need ironing in my closet, plus the labels "absent minded" and "improvident/reckless".

Young kids get dirty a lot by default—we must accept it as normal. So why then do all parents, especially Moms, tend to get so angry when that happens? Probably because they will have to do laundry again, or because the neighbours never see their kids clean and . . . shock and horror! They will get the name of uncaring mothers! So, the child gets shouted at, insulted, and sometimes slapped. And the poor little thing wonders what the heck is going on . . . Clumsiness is inherent in their age, but the child is not aware of it—how could they know it? Again, it is the mother's anger that is more important to them, the words with which she describes them, and I've heard whatnot—from "why can't you stay clean for five minutes" to "look at you—you are a pig".

For a long time, I have been wearing dark clothes—black, dark blue, brown. Guess why? Every time I liked a white, yellow, pink or light blue dress, my Mom would intercept my desire with the words "you . . . in white?" with the respective intonation, of course. This was not a question, it was a statement. I knew very well what she meant.

I started wearing light-coloured clothes when I could buy them myself, free from Mom's disapproving look. And don't think I became particularly deft, adroit and un-messy—hardly so. I remember having a favorite white skirt as a student at college—I hardly wore it dry, as I always managed somehow to pour coffee or coca cola all over it and had to rush to the nearest sink to wash it as it was—on me. Maybe the label "clumsy" had become my second nature, stronger than myself, and after each gaffe, I consolidated it myself.

I realized nagging didn't work when my elder daughter said one day ". . . since everybody thinks I'm lazy . . ." Not that it wasn't true, but after that statement, I realized that we have gone a bit too far with the nagging and have actually labeled her. If you think she bothered to prove us wrong, you are wrong. Just the opposite, she continued to laze about, probably thinking that no matter what she did, she'd hardly manage to change our opinion of her. She simply decided to live up to the image we have so tactlessly helped her build.

Third Mistake

Jumping to conclusion about the intellectual or artistic potential of the child.

„Ivan is good at mathematics, but he can't handle reading and writing", „Maria is very bad at singing or drawing"—you have probably heard many times similar remarks from concerned parents. We are fast to attach labels at the very first attempts our kids make in any area, not realizing that skills and abilities are learnt and developed. Our premature conclusions stop them in the bud. Not everyone is born with a talent but each and everyone of us can acquire and develop well skills in every area, as long as our efforts are recognized and appreciated and we are encouraged, instead of being written off with our first or second failure.

Fourth Mistake

Broken balance between criticism, punishment and praise and reward.

In order to avoid the two extremes whereby you either create a domineering despot, who shows no respect for you and is convinced that you are supposed to serve them, or you create a timid, insecure person who can easily be controlled and manipulated, you've got to find the necessary balance between criticism and praise, punishment and reward.

When the child misbehaves, punish them. But do not offend them, pouring down negative epithets over them, especially if you are out of the house. When the punishment is "served", and your anger has subsided, talk to the child calmly. Explain why he/she should not do or behave the way he/she did, what is unacceptable in his/her behaviour, what bothers or hurts you. And by no means, force them into promising "that it won't happen again". Just remember how many times in your childhood you made that promise, only to failed to fulfill it, and you will understand how pointless this responsibility is for the little person.

And remember: when you dump all your anger on the child, you create a guilt complex in them as they love you unconditionally and suffer that they made you angry.

Another mistake is to let good deeds go unnoticed. Yes, for us—adults, they are normal and we do not pay much attention to them, but they are important to the child, who is learning to discern between good and evil. If they don't get praised, in their mind they will belittle the good deed. And as children need to seek the attention of adults, they will get into more mischief that is sure to get a reaction from us, their good deeds will happen less and less often as they don't attract our attention.

To illustrate this, let me tell you about the answer of a mother of three on the matter:

When her daughter asked her:

- *Mom, you almost never notice my success and my good deeds, but when I do something wrong—you are always there to reproach me or punish me. Why is that?*

Her Mom replied:

- *At the street lights, when you cross the street as you should, does the policeman come to pat you on the shoulder and say "well done! You cross the street very well"? No, right? He comes when you are in violation, to fine you."*

Fifth Mistake

Breaking the natural hierarchy.

The natural hierarchy tends to be broken when the child has been waited for, for a long time or is adopted. Striving to give their best, some parents place themselves in service of the child to such an extent that the child grows up thinking he/she is the master. And they ARE the actual master of the house. It is the parents who place themselves in the role of staff and then in a few years time, they complain to friends and family that their kids show no respect for them and treat them as second-hand people.

You may always wish to respond to the wishes of the little crybaby, but if you do not refuse them things from time to time, he/she will grow up convinced that anything goes. And you will be the first to taste the bitter fruits of the broken hierarchy in the relationship with your kids. For whatever you sow in early childhood, so shall you reap later in adulthood.

I guess this is nothing new, it's a truism, yet the purpose of the "label removal" process is to uncover these little seeds in our memories and consciously pluck them out, no matter how much they have overgrown.

EXERCISE
The Garden—Flowers and Weed

Imagine that the soul of your child is a garden in which you have sown different quality (according to you) seeds. You observe the seeds sprouting out of the soil with a sense of contentment and fulfillment. They grow and develop and then suddenly . . . surprise, surprise—among the noble growth, you find weed. How did it get there? It is easier, of course, to blame the kid's friends who, according to you, exert bad influence on him/her; the environment—the kindergarten or school; the Internet, where kids come across all kinds of information and often entertain themselves with games, in which violence abounds; or older brother or sister who are unacceptable role models. And you—where are you in the whole picture? I think, you can answer this one for yourself, if only you thought about your own behaviour, your way of interaction and communication, the values and principles, to which you stick or often ignore.

If you are a parent and you have noticed characteristics—weeds in your child, do all you can to pluck them out before they have grown too deep a root and have overgrown to the point of suffocating the noble traits of character and preventing them from developing—let's call them flower-traits.

Note: The phrase "do all you can" excludes violence.

If you are an adult and want to handle the weed-traits, your battle shall first have to go through awareness with relation to the factors which helped their formation and development through the years. To be able to do this, you will have to go back to your childhood and remember a number of events, even the ones that you thought insignificant. If you are wondering how an insignificant event could have affected you so much, look at the graphic presentation of the process we gave at the beginning of the book:

Judgments=>labels=>beliefs=>personal qualities=>success/failure

So, you have made up your mind to take care of the weeds from your childhood. Start mentally plucking them out from the garden of your soul. In time, some of them will reappear because they have not been completely uprooted. Pluck them out again, and again, and again—visualize the weeding of the garden, until you get rid of them completely, until your soul is completely weed-free.

This small exercise can be done in the evening, before going to sleep, or in the morning—right after waking up, when your brain is still in alpha state. You have probably heard that this state between the wakefulness and the sleep is most productive in relation to storing up new knowledge. It is then that the new suggestions, through which you wish to change something in yourself, have a chance to be planted in your conscious and subconscious mind.

It will be even better if you have a real garden. While weeding it, imagine that each weed you pluck out of the ground, is one of your flaws with which you wish to part, "pluck it out" of your character.

WheN we aRe coMPaRed . . .

Negative comparisons with brothers or sisters, close kin and acquaintances rather hurt the dignity of the child than encourage them to catch up with the praised person.

Adults sometimes fail to notice that the child is in the room when they discuss them with other adults. Perhaps we don't realize how our discussion of their acts and skills with other people, which the child does not perceive as close, is going to affect them. They may feel betrayed, belittled, criticized or publicly reproached. Outside the family, in the strictest sense of the phrase, the child feels on foreign ground—unprotected and vulnerable. Bear that in mind next time you decide to share with somebody the child's difficulties in acquiring new skills and knowledge and your difficulties in the process of raising them! Look around you, and if the little guy is near, put off the conversation for a more appropriate time.

Comparison is especially detrimental to the child's fragile psyche. We all maintain that we love our kids equally, yet we constantly point out their differences in front of them with a shade of judgment. How can the child build up his/her self-esteem when they hear all the time "look how well your brother/sister is doing (with his/her studies, with the fork and knife, in sports and other activities), and you just flop/lag behind". You can guess what the outcome would be.

The same mechanism is triggered when we compare our kids with the neighbours' child, a schoolmate, etc.

It's an established fact that low self-esteem may lead to aggression or self-destructive behaviour. The "praised one" may later be harassed and insulted with or without reason, and may even get slapped by your otherwise quiet son or daughter. This option is preferable as aggression is taken out of the system, it is out in the open and sounds the alarm that something is wrong with your child's peace of mind, so that you, as a caring parent, may seek specialized help in order to handle their unacceptable behaviour. The less preferable option is when the child directs the aggression inwards, at themselves because it is often then, that psychosomatic diseases occur, they may hurt themselves, or take excessive risks, or start thinking about death or even attempt suicide in the worst case scenario.

Many of us carry the heaviest and most permanent labels from this period of our lives when they were attached by adults (parents, relatives, teachers), comparing us to people we had thought our equals, but placing us beneath them.

There are no such statistics (nobody thought of doing it), but life has proven that a very small percentage of successful people have been motivated to develop their skills this way—by constantly hearing how someone, such as their closest person, is better, more talented, smarter and superior at almost everything. The huge percentage of suppressed, de-motivated and insecure people turned that way ALSO because of negative comparisons to which they had been subjected in their childhood.

Let us consider the other extreme in the children-parents relationship, as the building up of excessively high self-esteem in children at the age of 0 to 7 is no less harmful for them. If you put the little prince or princess on a pedestal at their earliest age, they are sure to come crushing down with the first days at school. Because they are going to find themselves in the company of many other princes or princesses, with whom they will have to compete for territory—in their case—for the attention of the teacher or for the psychological or physical dominance over their classmates.

How would they feel tumbling down from such a height? Many of those kids will never feel "Number One" in their life again, they may even never want to be at the top again because of fear and shame of failure. Inside, they may feel they are the best, but without the recognition of others, they will feel misunderstood and unhappy.

WheN we coMPaRe ouRseLves . . .

Imagine how from the very first day at school, right to the Prom day, in the course of over a decade, we all take part in a beauty, intellect, talent and skills contest. And no one is equally good in all areas, but at first we all strive to be perfect in everything. We gradually find out what we are good at, and what we are not so good at. But, when we go to school, we carry our prevalent attitude, passed on to us by our family. Some of us highlight and are proud of the things we are good at, but talk halfheartedly of our failures, and inside our minds we consciously ignore them. Others, do just the opposite—they turn their failures into a drama, blame themselves (and if someone else blames them too—just watch . . .), yet they take their successes for granted as if no attention should be paid to them. They are not especially happy with their success because they are too busy eating themselves from the inside. Thus, the constant grinding of their failures turns into a habit at a certain point (also see the chapters on Habits and Failures). So, they attach their own negative labels and the more they chew and dissect their failures mentally, the bigger their insecurity gets and the more they get to doubt their intellectual and physical abilities.

Too often is the reason for our dissatisfaction with ourselves hidden in comparisons we make between ourselves and our classmates. We are still not mature enough to appreciate that people are different, that no two people are equally good or bad in all spheres of knowledge or in handling mundane problems.

During the first school years, the child is still in "I want" mode. They don't know their limits yet and want to be the best in everything. This is especially true of the favoured children in the family.

At this stage, the support of the parents is crucial as they can protect the child from serious psychological breakdowns with patience and love. Not only can they, but they are obliged to not allow single, or a series of failures in a given area to undermine the self-esteem of their child. Yes, some are better at Mathematics, others at drawing, or the Humanities. But each capability, or skill, can be developed with perseverance. Punishment, insults or comparisons with the top of the class in a given subject will not help, but they will sure stick a label in the kid's mind which the child will carry for years.

Later, during the teenage years, our comparison with other people takes a different turn. Our appearance, the clothes we wear, the accessories, hair, etc., become more important to us than our success at school, or rather the word "success" changes its meaning for us at this age.

Well, we drive our parents crazy when they watch us spend hours in front of the mirror, tending to our hair, trying new hair styles, instead of studying, but that's what they are there for—to grumble. At that age, to be beautiful, to attract attention, to be cool, is more important to us.

The boys in turn, strive to build biceps and abdominal plates, some of them are fond of martial arts and other sports, developing strength and agility. And in their striving for physical perfection, school, of course, remains entirely in the background.

It takes time before we stop trying to imitate other people, just because they are popular, and find our own style. Imitation and mimicry are common among young children and teenagers, but it should not turn into a means to an end in itself. They take any criticism too emotionally, even innocent comments may cause a disproportionately violent reaction, and thus labels stick easier to their fragile psyche.

The School—a Factory for Labels

Perhaps we should start from the kindergarten where each one of us faces judgment from others (outside the circle of our parents and close relatives) for the first time, as well as comparisons and competition with peers. Mom and Dad are not there to lend a helping hand when you are in need of support—you are on your own.

But let's skip it and start our analysis with the schools years. The situation is pretty much the same, but the responsibilities of the little person sharply increase from day one at school. If the child is the little darling at home, at school they have to compete with around 20 other children for the attention and approval of the teacher. The child will have to prove that they are up to speed with those 20 peers and to either become friends with them, or a leader. In an environment with so many competitors, it is extremely rare that they all like you and accept you.

Some children become victims of their more aggressive peers—unfortunately, it usually is the well-behaved, quiet and good children. Once the bullies get away with it, it happens again and again, until it turns into constant harassment.

The labels a bullying peer can attach to their victim, are countless—"pussy, wimp, nerd, pretentious, loser", etc. This is the age when we get mostly labels, related to our physique.

Stick, Lollipop (Irish), **Lumpy, Blob, or Heifer** (Irish)—weight related;

Baldie or Kojak (Irish) and Wooly or Curlylocks (Irish)—hair, related;

"Blind as a bat", "Googy eyes", "Goggled-eyes", "Frog-eyes" (Irish), Specky-four-eyes (British), Cross-eyed, Cock-eyed, Loving Eyes—related to the eyes and wearing glasses;

Booger Boy, Sniveller, Germy, Smelly Pants (Irish), **Stinker** (Irish)—for sickly children or children with poor hygiene;

Twin Tower, Big Bird, Jolly Green Giant, Peanuts, Shorty, Itty-bitty, Shrimpy and Midget—height related;

Bucky, Buck, Beaver, Rabbit, Splinter, Goofy, (Irish), **Braces**—for problem teeth and braces—in this respect, kids are very inventive.

Every physical peculiarity is commented with a shade of the grotesque.

And nothing helps—neither complaining to the teacher, nor to the parents. Things may even get worse if a parent decides to intervene—in 90 % of the cases, nicknames are more likely to stick rather than fade with time.

The law of the jungle is in full swing—growing up, we learn to survive, to impose on others, or not allow others to impose on us. Brute force is not always the solution, though.

As I go back to my childhood, I think that none of my nicknames stuck longer than a week. Why was that? Probably because I fought every word spoken about me, regardless whether it was related to my appearance or my character. They did not even dare call me a "bully". Simply, at one point they stopped bothering me. I had proved strong enough not to let them victimize me. It was as if I had stuck a sign on me: "Do not touch me!", but then—later I suffered that people had difficulties getting close to me, and I to them.

Now, from the distance of time, I think that I probably needed specialized help, but obviously none of the adults around me saw things that way—they just satisfied themselves with the statement "she is a handful", "tough puberty" and other such . . . I was a rebel, but my classmates hardly realized that my strength to confront not only them, but our teachers as well, was not some exceptional quality of character, but rather a compensational mechanism, through which my psyche was trying to regain its balance. I didn't have many of the things that they had. In the first place, I didn't have a healthy family at a time when "divorcee" was a stigma, not something trivial. I wasn't the darling of the family, my parents were poor, fashion was not something my Mom could afford to be interested in, so I don't care much about it to this day, although I can now afford to buy all the clothes I want. I had to regain the balance of which circumstances had deprived me.

From that period I carry the labels of "a rebel", "different", "hard to integrate", "independent", "confrontational", "disrespectful of authority". Some of them I still like, others are still in the way, no matter what the working environment.

Labels are given to us not only by our peers but by teachers as well. We can't blame them as they are human too—they have their biases, likes and dislikes. They "pay their dues" to our load of labels. What is worse—our parents do it, and later on we do it ourselves—we very obligingly transfer the teachers' labels after each parent-teacher meeting. Perhaps, we should learn to hold back some of the information received from the teachers about our kids. We are not helping them much when we repeat the reproaches of the teachers word by word.

So, if you have young children, think about it. It would be easier for you to understand what I mean if you go back to your own school years—there is no way you have gotten out of that period without at least one label. If you have a specific incident, especially if it's a repeating one—a particular word that the teacher used to characterize you, think what it might have been if your parents had withheld it. Wouldn't you have felt differently, wouldn't your development have taken a different turn—a more favourable one? Now imagine that coming back from the parent-teacher meeting, your parent gave you only the positive feedback from the teachers and spared you the negative. Wouldn't you try to deserve the praise?

You don't have to lie to your children, but it's very unnecessary, even harmful to share with them the following: "your teacher thinks you are lazy". Isn't it enough that your child hears this judgment from you several times a day? Or do you need the support of the teachers' authority to make your child listen to you? I am sure you provide good advice, and just want the good of your child, but transferring the teachers' reproach in the family is definitely not the best approach.

Find another way to motivate your child to change some of their habits, behaviour, or the organization of their training process. The feedback from the teachers is for you, its purpose is to give you hints as to what to work on with your child, not to pass on it to the child word for word.

The same holds true for praise—no matter how happy it made you, be moderate when you share it with your child.

And a little side note: refrain from comments on the child's classmates, never mind whether we are talking about praise or complaints from teachers. Because, the very next day, they will all share who said what about whom, and you will get them into an intrigue which they are not ready to handle yet.

Nicknames—Teenage Teasing or a Stigma?

Have you ever heard of nicknames, such as Smarty pants, The Beauty, the Handy one, whose owner is really smart, beautiful or skilled? No, right?

Nicknames usually refer to the absence of positive traits in the individual or the abundance of a certain negative trait—whether it refers to the appearance or character specifics.

So, it is because of that, that nicknames such as Crookey, The Bat, Stuttering Stanley and other such, referring to the physical specifics of its owner, abound.

Nicknames like Grumpy, grumbler, Grouch, Bellyacher, Crybaby, Phoney, Fibber, Trickster, Spoofer, Blagger, (Irish), Blunderer, Duffer, and Looser, refer to the character and behavior of the person who acquired them.

Nicknames are also labels, and tend to stick longer, following their owner for years. People often think that when they change their school, or start a new job, they will leave their nickname behind. Alas, this is rarely the case—created as a joke, the label turns into a stigma. There's always someone in your new circle, or your new work place, who is a friend of a friend in your old neighbourhood, neighbour of your cousin . . . and the nickname catches up with you. It may not be present in your new life as strongly as before, but it inevitably resurfaces, as if from nowhere, if you offend or step on the toes of your new colleagues or friends.

There are nicknames which disappear with time. But even though you may not hear them anymore, if they carried a negative charge for you, they traumatized your confidence and you buried them deep inside as live charcoal buried in ashes. Is it worth digging them?

The answer is not unequivocal. If you have already forgotten them, allow them to fade away undisturbed. If you feel, though, that they have somehow changed your destiny, that they have diverted you from the chosen path, go back and try to remember in as much detail as possible, the situation that created them, and the feelings that the very mention of your nickname arose in the beginning, when you still resisted your given label. That is where the process of removal should begin. Recognize to what extent you—with your actions, gestures or habits, have caused the invention of your nickname, and to what extent the person, who turned out to be particularly resourceful at your expense, had acted out of envy, spite, rivalry and desire to hurt, debase and ridicule you.

Simply accept the fact that not everyone can like you—neither now nor before, and that's not necessary.

Forgive the joker and forget them—together with their ridiculous witticism. If you still haven't turned that page of your life, do it now.

Authority Figures

Everybody has authority figures in his life—people whose opinion is especially important for him, but at the same time each one of us is an authority figure within our own circle. Even if it is only for our children, it is still a part of the labeling game.

How long will a label stick in our subconsciousness depends on how high the pedestal, on which we have placed our authority figures is. An innocent remark from such a person, even when it is completely devoid of any desire on their behalf to hurt us, but was rather meant as advice, may exercise influence over us for years, even for life. Even a joke, or an invention . . . the latter does not happen to everyone, but it did to me. It was in my adult years that I realized how a joke, invented by my mother, had "twisted" me, and all of a sudden, a number of emotional reactions in my childhood, and even later—in my relationships with other people, became clear to me.

The Mother Figure

I hope you would agree that the mother is the first authority figure for the child. My apologies to fathers, but I think generally, they intervene in the child-rearing, development and personality formation of their offspring at a much later stage.

Children usually ask questions to their mothers about the events around their birth—at the early age of 3 to 5, I can't really determine the exact age—it is different for everyone. In any case, this is not just curiosity. The child, becoming aware of the fact that it is a separate individual, seeks its "beginning".

Here is the invented story my mother used to tell me:

> When I was born, I was black and ugly. And because of that, my mother entered into an argument with a gypsy woman who

maintained that I was her daughter. Each of the two women claimed me, and in the end my mother prevailed. You realize that when you are 3 or 5, there is no way you can know that when a mother lays eyes on her newly born baby for the first time, there is no way she would mistake it for another, even though the two babies may be like two peas in a pod—it's the Moms' instinct. Well, I realized that much later . . . when I had my own children.

As far as I remember, we had a lot of fun with that story. But . . . repeated numerous times, it definitely gave me the labels "black" and "ugly" from my earliest childhood, especially in combination with the explanation that my sister was "white and beautiful" when she was born.

I realize that telling this story may make my mother seem like a monster. But she wasn't. I think, she simply tried to get something out of me—obedience, based on gratitude that she had prevailed in the argument over me and the fact that I live in decent conditions rather than in a gypsy camp. Or she probably wanted to cool down my rebellious nature by undermining my confidence . . . I don't really know, I never asked her while she was alive what the purpose of this inappropriate joke really was.

My sister was a timid child, and a diligent student—she obviously did not need such emergency measures. And as far as I remember—both the praise and the reproach were well deserved by us.

After many years, I realized that we are both equally "black" and "white", "beautiful" and "ugly"—after all, beauty is in the eye of the beholder. On top of that, when we were teenagers, people often thought we were twins, maybe because of the small age difference between us. Only, I had inferiority complexes, and she did not. The labels my mother had given me for some reason known only to her had stuck and affected me.

The FatheR FiguRe

The authority of the father is based mostly on physical strength and intellect. He is the strong one, the clever one, the one from whom the child expects protection and answers to every question. But fathers have this strange inclination to spoil their daughters and treat their sons harshly. Thus, girls turn into Dad's princess, and boys are mostly required to develop strength, agility, resilience and emotional restraint. But the little child is not a man yet, as Daddy wishes—the little guy still needs warmth, consolation and caresses. Crying is still an instinctive reaction to pain and insult, and the mother immediately, instinctively takes up the role of a consoler. It is then that the 3, 4 or 5 year old man may receive the labels "weakling", "pussy", "Mommy's boy", which he will try to run away from in the following years. Whether he will remain a "weakling" and a "pussy", or he will turn into a ruffian, and a bully, depends on many factors in his personal life, but the seed of doubt in his masculinity is already sown in his heart by his own father.

The TeacheRs

At 7, you can hardly judge whether you stand in front of a devoted tutor or a half-hearted official, or a pedophile (there are such cases, lets not kid ourselves). Teachers become authority figures for us at an early age and their opinion/judgment is important to us. Mom and Dad entrusted us to them, right?—we have to do what they tell us, respect them, obey them. And if one of them told you "don't be such a bully?", even if you don't know what that means, you know that you are in trouble by the tone of voice.

Those early school years are even harder for the boys. A boy trips and falls, hurts his knee and begins to cry. But Mom and Dad are not around to console him, and the teacher or supervisor, who is responsible for 20 more kids, blurts out "Come on now, don't cry, you are not a girl, are you? Be a man", or worse yet "stop that baby stuff".

If you are wondering why men cry only at funerals, and even then they try to restrain their feelings, this is the answer—they try to escape the labels, related to feminine behaviour and immaturity.

Teachers manage to give us a number of other labels, such as "lazy", "absent minded", "unreliable", "aggressive", etc. To what extent these labels will hurt us also depends on our parents (see the Parents chapter).

The good news is that the influence of the teacher authority figures diminishes as students grow up. Or maybe, that's bad news, I don't know . . .

The fact is that as they grow up, young people rely more and more on their inner guiding system rather than on external factors.

Only, we have been programmed in such a way as to allow the continued parade of authority figures . . .

The Leader of the Pack

Each group of 15-16 or 20-year olds has its informal leader. Nobody elected them, they established themselves and their opinion matters. This is the person who might give you a label. If you are the leader, your judgments, spoken accidentally, innocently or on purpose, may turn into labels which would remain in your friends' minds even after your group has scattered.

Very often these groups have several candidates for the leadership place who throw labels at each other, play pranks to each other, manipulate the rest of the members of the group in one direction or another. And this goes on until the candidates strike a bargain between themselves, and a hierarchy of sorts is established within the group. It is not always the best person who manages to establish himself as a leader, sometimes, the best manipulator has the better chances to influence the rest, to attract them to his ideas and often, to use them for his own purposes.

The EMPLoyeR, the CoLLeagues

If your employer is not an authority figure for you, you would simply not choose him, and would not apply for a job in his company. And as you have chosen to work for him, his feedback will diminish or uplift you—in your own mind, of course, as his game may be an entirely different story—i.e. your employer will be the one to give you labels. I wish you get only positive ones.

If you feel depressed at work, though, expecting to be criticized by your boss at any minute for some minute omission, and at the same time failing to notice your good performance, then that means that you have found yourself in the hands of a manipulator, who has chosen this way to control his subordinates, or simply, you should not be in this company. The faster you quit, the quicker you will forget the unjust reproaches and will not allow them to turn into labels.

The same advice holds true with relation to your colleagues. You may ignore for a certain period of time the intrigues, in which you are involved, but how long can you play deaf and dumb? If they play nasty tricks on you, if they do backbiting, if they try to take credit for things you have done (and at the same time highlight your faults in front of your boss), is it worth breaking a sweat for them and going home after work tired like a dog, emotionally drained from it all? And all this—day after day, month after month, for years . . .

The InTiMate PaRtNeR oR SPouse

Now this is where, you might get in real trouble.

Love is blind, or at least it makes us believe that there is a great chance that we might make the compromise and accept and get used to the flaws of our beloved. In the long run, though, these seemingly trifle things turn into causes of everyday arguments and insults, which are only half a step away from the labels. And we walk that half step the minute we realize that a certain word, expression or behaviour particularly hurts the other. The worst is that we start taking advantage—as some form of self defense we press the button which activates the negative label we had given our partner or the one they had been carrying since before they met us, again and again.

What we activate may be a specific qualifier, or a state of mind—anger, insult, helplessness, depression, dependence, etc., and we manipulate it, thus making our partner feel bad. Do we feel better for that? I don't think so. But the strategy is infallible—press the button, activate the label, trigger the respective reaction, our partner is out of balance, sometimes to the extent that they forget the reason for the argument. We feel stronger, more convincing, and even the arguments in favour of our rightness become redundant. Victory! Well, a walkover . . . the power play within the couple is as pointless as it is old. It is instinctive for men and the result of emancipation for women. I wonder why we still keep on playing that game? What gives us power over the other? And finally, isn't the predominance, won that way, only a sign of our own weakness?

If we have positioned ourselves as the authority figure within the couple—we give the labels, if our partner is the one—we are the victims.

Balance almost does not exist in couples, except for the cases whereby one is an authority in one sphere, and the other—in another sphere. And it is still not a real balance. Or the more extreme case, where the relationship has turned into cohabitation with the roof and the habit as the only things in common.
Then we are completely protected from the labels because we are no longer interested in our partner's way of thinking.

Note: Read more on couple relationships in the next section.

There are numerous other authority figures in our life, but I do not aim to enumerate them here. What's common between them is the fact that we respect them and take their opinion of us personally, i.e. they are potential generators of labels which may haunt us for a long time.

EXERCISE

Downsizing the pedestal

As I mentioned in the beginning of this chapter, we tend to place authority figures on an imaginary pedestal—we are somewhere down there, at the bottom. Try to imagine them and let the height of the pedestal be proportional to their influence over you.

You will discover that some of them have become as high as you are—your work with them will be harder, but you should still try. Imagine that you are a child, they are "towering" over you and passing judgments, if it would be easier for you, imagine that instead of words, they are throwing stones (they have said many things but not all stones have hit you). When you manage to clearly "see" that picture in your mind, start downsizing their pedestal. Continue until it is as high as you are, if needed continue to do it until it is so small that you barely see it down there at your feet. Imagine that they continue to throw those stones—judgments-labels at you. What would you feel? Slight prickle or tickling in your feet, or ankles at best. By downsizing the pedestal of your authority figure, you neutralize the force with which the label, they have attached to you, affects you—you may feel it as a slight sting, which you can feel free to ignore.

(Figure 2)

As to the authority figures in your present life, you need not go back to your childhood. Do the above exercise and downsize the pedestal as much as YOU feel comfortable—i.e. to the height which will guarantee that the labels, which they try to attach to you, do not hurt you anymore. And the ones they have already succeeded in giving you, will disappear in time, as soon as you take away the pedestal from them.

What is Happening in My Life?

Friends

Have you ever thought why we take criticism coming from friends with so much ease? The answer is simple and easily reached by many of you—because in our relationships with friends, there is no hierarchy, we do not compete with them, they know all about us, we know all about them, our destinies are intertwined, and sometimes we perceive them as part of ourselves. I am talking of true friends.

Therefore, even if they sometimes criticize us, their criticism sounds like an advice to us, or like concern, and it is extremely rarely that it turns into a confidence-undermining label.

Friends can turn into your most valued assistants in the label-removing process. Make a list of the most hurtful labels, no matter who gave them to you—you, or someone else left them behind after a brief encounter in time, or as a result of longer cohabitation or cooperation. Show the list to your best friend (if you have more than one—even better—you will hear more than one opinion). You will be surprised how many labels from your list will emphatically be rejected by your friends as untrue, and for the remaining 10-20 percent, they will say "well, there's something like that in you but you sure overestimate its importance".

They will tell you that not because they love you and don't want to hurt you, but because indeed, the better part of the labels are only in your imagination, they are the load from your life experiences up to this moment, which you will have to shed, in order to be able to move on.

EXERCISE
The Backpack Full of Labels

Fill a backpack with unnecessary objects—the heavier they are, the better. On each object, stick a label, which prevents you from feeling good. Place at the bottom of the backpack the oldest ones, those from childhood, then from your teenage years, then from your first job, the beginning of your marriage, etc., etc . . . . until yesterday. Place them in this order—the oldest ones at the bottom, the latest ones on top. To do that, you need to make a list in advance and determine their chronology.

Even composing the list and the remembrance of the events from the past can help you realize that a specific statement had been imposed on you from outside, it had been a premature judgment of your abilities, but you were too immature and too emotional at the time, so you believed it. Then you consolidated it in the classical way—you expected it—from the same person or the same situation, and if you did not hear it again, you read it into other words and actions of the people around you, thus, you turned it into a label.

Are you ready with the backpack? If you are, pick it up. Walk around with it. Is it heavy? That is how your heart and soul feel under the burden of the labels, even though they are intangible. Walk around with your backpack long enough to remember the feeling. Now take out a couple of the objects at the top, bearing the labels you have received lately. Walk around again. It is easier now, isn't it? While walking, think—try to refute the labels that bother you, point out before yourself your opposite, positive qualities. You have them, don't doubt that. No one has only negative traits. Believe in your positive qualities and they will start manifesting more often in your reality.

This is the first stage of the exercise—it might take you a few days, or a week or two. Continue only after you manage to release the first couple of labels. You will feel lighter with every eliminated label. Your fears will leave you one by one, you will start living a fuller, more joyful life, and have more confidence in yourself.

Oh, yes, and you will improve your posture—this is a bonus many of us need.

Warning:
If you suffer from slipped discs, hernia, etc., the use of this method is inappropriate. Healing the soul should not be at the expense of damaging the body.

This EXERCISE can be done in a group as well.
Hiking with a backpack

A group of 10-12 people gather at the bottom of the mountain with empty backpacks and pieces of paper on which they have written their labels. The Organizer brings a number of wooden blocks (or bricks)—everybody sticks their labels on the blocks and arranges them in their backpack—the oldest—at the bottom, the most recent ones—on top. The participants walk along the path in complete silence (it is advisable that the path be a bit steep). While walking up the hill, the participants should observe their physical sensations and mentally counterattack some of their most recent labels. Well, it may happen that they mentally curse the Organizer of the exercise, or themselves for having subjected themselves to this ordeal, but this is a perfectly normal human reaction and they should not beat themselves up about it. In 45 minutes—a break. Sharing of thoughts and sensations during the climb. Then they are told that during the next 45 minutes they may unload part of their load, if it's too heavy, but with a ritual—by affirming mentally or aloud the opposite statement to the labels they are throwing out. Example: if the label is "indecisive", it should be thrown out with the words „I am decisive and resolute", if it is „stupid", the affirmation should be „I am smart".

Again 45 minutes of walking, and throwing out labels if necessary, repeating the ritual.

The Control Group consists of 3-4 persons, equal in physical abilities and training to the other participants. It should start 5 to 10 minutes earlier, and just like the group under observation, it will have 15-minute breaks every 45 minutes. They register how long it takes them to reach their target (for example, a mountain hut) and how tired they are.

The group under observation also registers the time it takes them to reach the target. Then the two groups get together and share thoughts, sensations, insights they've had while climbing up.

What do we prove with this exercise?—Something proved a long time ago—that when you carry a heavy load, you walk slower and with more efforts up the slope, as opposed to "travelling light". The analogy with our life experience is inevitable.

The purpose of the exercise is to feel the weight of the labels physically because this is the way to realize how much they are in your way, how exhausting it is to carry them around and how they slow you down on your way to achieving your goals in life. They are a useless burden, and you'll have to free your soul from it.

The Intimate Partner

Everything is great while we are getting to know each other. The problems start after that, when we have presumably accepted each other the way we are, especially after we start living under the same roof or get married.

The terrific, perfectly manicured young girl with great hair constantly turns into a shabby, disheveled, cantankerous and prematurely aged woman. While the irresistible macho, who used to steal the hearts of all women from 20 to 60, apart from the beer belly, walks around the house in his vest and underpants, stuffs himself with chips and ceaselessly drinks beer all through the week-end.

Physically, many of us have undergone this metamorphosis—some more, others—less so. More important is the psychological aspect of the change, though, the one that makes us confront each other in the power play. We then put to use the whole arsenal of means to belittle the other, brandish ourselves, give them a feeling of guilt, in order to make them feel grateful to us for putting up with them the way they are; to mend them because we know better what is good and what is bad; make them be afraid that we'll abandon them if they fail to fulfill our wishes; make them feel inferior and jealous, by sharing with them how many better options for an intimate partner we've had, but there you are—we were fooled by their kindness, they managed to deceive us, pretending to be better than they really are.

Labels are only a part of this arsenal. It is not necessary to voice them out as a concrete judgment of the qualities or flaws. Go through the following questions and statements and try to figure out the labels behind them:

> „Who do you think you are?"
> „You are lucky to have me—someone else wouldn't put up with you."
> „You'll never find anyone better than me"
> „What will you do without me?"
> „When will you grow up?"
> „Hasn't you mother taught you anything?"
> „Who gave you a driving license?"
> „You are no good."
> „I'm saying/doing that for your own good."
> „Stop bothering me with all this nonsense."
> „Haven't you given up that yet?"
> „Stop daydreaming."
> „If you love me, you would do x, y and z . . . (he/she can ask anything)."

And so on, and so forth . . .

As you probably have already noticed, most of the questions are not just questions—they are judgments, indignation with your flaws, requirements and attempts to degrade you and cool down your enthusiasm in pursuit of a certain goal. Spoken by the closest person, these judgments hurt, create complexes, hinder our future strives for expression, manipulate us, make us indecisive and weak. The better part of them would turn into labels which would, in turn, prevent us from developing our potential, realizing our dreams, feeling better in our own skin.

If we "peek" behind the words, these are masked demands, requirements of the other person to us, which we have failed to meet. Many couples make this mistake, instead of sitting down to talk and stating their requirements accurately and clearly.

D.M. 39 years old, *shared in the group that she has had a problem entering into a new relationship for three years now since her divorce. She was not doing anything to make herself more attractive to men because she thought she was "ugly, fat and old". Later on, we discovered that she had inherited these labels from her failed marriage, and she had accepted them to such an extent that she took them for granted. She had heard them many times from her ex-husband during almost every argument they'd had, and most frequently, in response to her declared desire to leave him. For us—people in the sidelines, it was clear that this was his defensive reaction to the risk of abandonment. But she had succumbed to his manipulations and the labels he had given her had become part of her perception of herself. Because she was neither ugly, nor fat. As to the label "old"—no comment needed.*

I'm just kidding . . .

Have you ever been in a situation where somebody offends you and then turns around and says: "What are you so uptight about . . . ? I was just kidding . . ." I'm sure you have. It usually comes from the people closest to us—our parents, siblings, friends, and later on our intimate partner. If you asked them about their motives, they would tell you that they were training your sense of humour, they were trying to help you overcome your excessive touchiness, and that they didn't mean to hurt you at all.

Yeah, right. If this is how they usually communicate, you should know that these are their complexes talking, only at your expense. You surpass them in something which they don't want to and never will admit. Or they want to dominate in your relationship, which they will not admit either.

If you are an adult, and this is a repeated model of communication between you and "the other one", next time, before you jump out of your skin and react the usual way, just ask them: "What? Kidding again?" I'm sure they will be stunned and will not know what to say. If, however, they manage to recover quickly, they will probably mumble "Yes, of course", but will realize that this time they didn't get away with it . . . well, probably next time they will try to be more resourceful, but in any case, you will have to learn to stand up for yourself. How? By letting them know that you take their words as a joke, though they secretly wound you. Because denigrating jokes (never mind in what area) are also labels that stick. And the closer the person who is "kidding" is to you, the stickier and harder to eliminate they may turn out to be.

At this point, we have to ask the following questions: What is a sense of humour? What is funny? Is there a universal criterion for fun? Why do people laugh at different things? When a joke wounds, is that funny? Is it fair to joke about something which is a complex for the other person? Where is the boundary between the innocent joke and the mockery? Perhaps the joker does not realize that he is stepping on our toes, that his joke is a blow below the waist?

Well, if he doesn't, it is time for him to know. Tell him, do not expect the other person to read your mind. Tell him: "This hurts because . . ." and state the reason.

Not always people want to hurt us, yet they do because they don't know what it is that wounds us. It is up to us to stop the out-of-line jokes about us instead of suffer needlessly.

S.K., 62 years old, has been happily married for almost 40 years. The only thing, she still has a problem accepting, is her husband's odd sense of humour. „His jokes are too savory—she says.—Sometimes he oversteps all boundaries, and I'm afraid that some of our friends may take offence and stop talking to us. Most of his friends are not angry, though, and respond in the same fashion. Take me, for example—I have taken offence many times and have stopped talking to him for days, but he is incorrigible. Once, I did not accompany him in his visit to some friends, and when they asked why I wasn't with him, he told them that I got so fat that I couldn't get through the door, and that's why I had to stay home. They know him well, yet they somehow fell for it. In a couple of months, the woman from that family met me on the street and said to me: "Crikey! You've lost so much weight!" I told her that in the past two years I've neither lost, nor gained weight. It was then that I understood what my dear husband had told them. When I asked him why he embarrassed me in front of people, he just laughed. Joker . . .

If this practice does not stop despite our efforts to explain to the other person that his jokes are inappropriate and hurtful to us, then we are talking about intentional attempts on their behalf to denigrate us, as well as attempts at manipulation, domineering, sometimes jealousy or fear of abandonment.

Is it often that we play "a Broken Telephone*"?

For a number of reasons, we sometimes hear things that our companion never even thought of saying.

If you decide to clarify the implied meaning for yourself and tell your companion what you have "heard", probably you will enter into a long, and basically pointless argument on the meaning of words, intonation, situations, etc . . . And if you are a married couple, you will inevitably end up discussing previous misunderstandings, you will start reproaching each other and before you know it—you will start throwing labels at each other which will easily stick to your agitated mind.

Important rule

The more emotionally charged a label, and the more agitated we are when attacked with it, the easier and better it sticks.

Is it better to keep silent and leave "the thing" to poison your mind? For the time being—yes. But by all means, clarify with the other person, when you are both CALM, whether the implied meaning you "heard" is not a figment of your imagination, old trauma (not necessarily inflicted

---

*   This is a children's game, also known in some countries as "Russian Telephone". A group of kids line up and a message is whispered into the ear of the first in line, who is supposed to pass it on by whispering it to the next in line and then the next . . . and they do so until the message gets to the last one. The last kid then speaks out loud what he has heard and usually it has nothing to do with the original message. Then they trace the message back and find out where the line has broken.

by the same person), your low self esteem, or your overall attitude towards this person or the subject of the conversation.

More on what people are saying to us, and what we are "hearing", read in the next chapter, as well as in the chapters "Words are to be Blamed for Everything" and "Suspicion".

Other People's Resistance—or "I Remove them, he/she sticks them back"

The minute you start "unpacking" and getting rid of your labels, even if you don't say a word to anybody, you should expect resistance from outside with the first positive results. The people around you, who have more or less contributed to your labeling, will immediately sense the change of your energy, and will attempt to restore the status quo. Not knowing the reasons, they will feel you slip out of their control, and their well ordered life (which suits them perfectly) will be shaken. They may love you very much and care about you, but the change in you will disturb and confuse them, and may seem to them as some vague threat . . . to their own confidence, of course. They may even resume the attack against you with old or new labels.

Others tend to perceive you as some fixed set of qualities, flaws, reactions, habits and beliefs. This is what they call "getting to know the person." They know you and have accepted you as you are, they know what your reaction would be in a number of situations, even what you would say or think on a particular occasion. In case they have not completely accepted you as you are, they try to mend you. Yet, even though they have insisted that you changed something in yourself, such as reactions, views, or habits, the minute you really start changing, be it under the influence of this, or another similar book, or because you don't like some aspect of yourself and have decided to change it, they stand on the alert. They begin to doubt that they have known you all that well, and this makes them feel insecure, uncomfortable, and the puzzle of which you are a part, is slightly misplaced. It is only natural that they would want to restore things to the previous balanced (according to them) state.

If this is your spouse, the change in you may seem to them like a threat. Well, magazines for men and women, which periodically publish articles of the "Ten Signs that He/She is Unfaithful to You" type, also contribute to the situation—by rule, every change is interpreted as a sign of unfaithfulness in these articles.

Example 1

A slipshod, sloppy housewife all of a sudden decides to go to the hairstylist, to have a manicure, to play sports or go on a diet. It does not necessarily mean that another male has attracted her attention. Maybe she got tired of being the way she was, so she decided to make the change—for herself, for others, for more positive emotions, for more confidence.

Even with the smallest change in his partner, the man is on the alert, feeling threatened. If he is not the rough and despotic type who would ask "Who are you powdering up for?", most probably his compliments would be poisonous, something like "You are OK, no need to lose weight" or "What have you done to your hair? You look like our neighbour so and so", believe me, he will choose the neighbour whom he knows you can't stand, or the one that is openly hostile to you.

Another version is "You are going to play sports? At your age?" or "Are you planning to stop cleaning and washing at home?", referring to your new manicure, and ultimately your overall makeover: "Perhaps we should hire help, if you intend to be dressed up for the opera all the time!"

Did you hear the labels your beloved does not want you to remove, by making these remarks accidentally, or on purpose?

You are fat.
You are clumsy and sloppy.
You are old.
You are lazy.
You are the maid at home.

Yes, you heard something about opera, but it was not an invitation. Well, you invite him if you can swallow his offensive and mocking attitude towards your desire to change.

Example 2

A middle-aged man decided to play sports, to dress neatly although his job did not require a special dress code, but what the heck—let's put some of the New Year's gifts to use. The reason may be a new female colleague but not necessarily. The decision to change does not always have to be the result of external factors.

Instead of being happy that at last her "instructions" bear fruit, his wife feels threatened and in her head . . . big-bosomed blondes drive her crazy . . . remarks of the following sort: "Since when do you shave every day?", "This belly will take years to get rid of and you still won't look the way you did 20 years ago" are only the light artillery from the arsenal of the suspicious woman. He decides to change the bulbs in the corridor and unclog the sink because finally, these trifles got to him as well, but his wife follows him around muttering "All that fawning, we'll see what will come out of it . . ." And it's a good day if she doesn't comment: "Finally! A man in the house!"

Did you "hear" the labels behind these remarks?

You are careless and negligent to yourself.
You are fat and sloppy.
You are old.
You do not perform your duties as a man at home.
You are a schmuck.

Friends, or the usual companions, may play the same role—pull you back and try to prevent the change.

Example 3

You have decided to cut down on cigarettes, or give them up completely. If you insist on continuing to meet with your usual companions, prepare to face difficulties in following up on your intentions to make a change in your life.

You meet some of them and, you do not light a cigarette the first 5 minutes, you do not do it in the following 15 minutes. One of them notices and is puzzled: "Don't tell me you've given up smoking . . ." It doesn't matter what your reply would be, he'll probably add: "I've tried many times but it doesn't work, bro, it's for the strong of will". If you tell him that you haven't given up smoking, but you still don't light a cigarette, he'll probably offer you most sincerely: "Here, have some of mine if you don't have any, if you've got no money, I'll lend you some."

Do an experiment and refrain from smoking until the end of this meeting. In 7 out of 10 similar cases, your friend will be concerned and ask before you part: "Are you ill or something? Did the doctors forbid you to smoke?" he will do it, not realizing that he tries to get you back to a place you've decided to leave. Maybe because he'll feel a bit lonely in his vice, it would seem to him that you are moving apart, or maybe he is sincerely concerned about your health. In any case, the balance in your relationship will be shaken a bit, even by such a small change. Perhaps he will decide to support you next time you see each other, if he is a true friend. But at first, he will feel a bit uncomfortable and refuse to accept the change that is happening with you.

And did you "hear" the labels?

You are a chain smoker.
You have no willpower.
It is only by force (disease or poverty) that you would give up this harmful (but so sweet) habit.

The same example can refer to the attempts to give up or reduce alcohol abuse.

There are other specific qualities of ours without which even the well-meaning friends have difficulty accepting us. We are so locked within the stereotype—I am talking of all of us, that we have difficulty accepting even the smallest change in the other and, in most cases, it seems to us incidental.

For years I could not get rid of my habit to be late. I made efforts, of course, but when I managed to get to the meeting on time, even before I had time to congratulate myself on my punctuality, I used to hear the comment: „Well done, for once you are on time." It so happened that the other party was also late sometimes, and guess what the excuse was "I know you are never on time, so I decided there was no point to be in such a hurry". And so, the label "always late" haunted me through the years. Not that I did not deserve it, but the few breaks of habit that I managed to achieve crashed into the frozen idea about me I had managed to give others, which now hampered the change I so wanted to make, rendered my efforts pointless and finally undermined my motivation.

The same happens with the comments about my weight. More than two years have passed since I shed around 10 kg, but it happens at least once a fortnight that someone would compliment me on losing weight. These come from people who see me twice a month, or at least—every couple of months. It seems that the image of a chubbier me has stuck in their minds to such an extent that they refuse to accept my new, slimmer me. The label "fat" does not suit my figure any more but somehow, unconsciously (I hope it is) my friends activate it in my mind.

THOUGHT EXPERIMENT
The Website

Imagine that you are a website. What would your tags/keywords (labels) be, so that the search engines (Google, Yahoo, etc.) can find you easily? Probably they will reflect your distinctive features, characteristics in your appearance and behaviour. Visualize the people with whom you interact on a day-to-day basis or incidentally in the role of the search engines. Do not be fooled—in most cases, strangers have some preliminary information about you before they come into contact with you—these are your tags and keywords, which have become known to them in one way or another.

Your relatives, friends and brief acquaintances have also put tags on you and have arranged you in their mind according to their own classification. Don't you believe it? Try to describe with a few words one of your close friends or relatives—handsome, ugly, vicious, smart, lazy, dreamer—these are his tags. And we all have them. Some of them we accept, others hurt us, but they are like levers for others, which help them develop their attitude towards us. (In the case of our self imposed tags—they determine our self-esteem and our perception of ourselves.)

When we start changing, we start to correspond less and less to our tags (the labels others gave us rightly or wrongly), and it is perfectly normal for the people who've known us for a long time, to start wondering what's got into us. They often start to ask themselves whether they've ever known us well enough—it may seem to them that up to that moment we have pretended, we have played some role. We make things difficult for them—their "search engine" does not find us through the old tags and key words, they have to think of new ones, and it takes a long time for them to sink in. Why does their resistance to our change surprise us then?

When we have labeled ourselves, changes confuse us too—our own "search engine" is having a hard time. During the "Label Removing" process, we often ask ourselves—are we good or bad, smart or stupid, because in our mind, the old and the new perceptions of ourselves will collide. This will put some stress on us, and stress—if allowed—will pull us back into our comfort zone, to the old labels.

That is why perseverance during the "Label Removing" process is key to the change we yearn.

The MotheR iN Law

Although there are more jokes about his mother-in-law than hers, his mother-in-law is more harmless than hers when it comes to label sticking and systematic psychological harassment. It may be so because by rule men don't take "women's talk" so personally, and do not consider themselves less deserving than the mother of their spouse.

The young and the older woman, though, when put in the "in-law" situation, from the very first moment turn into rivals, competing for the heart, attention and influence over the beloved man. Sometimes the struggle is open, sometimes subversive. He finds himself in the middle of all this and by rule, does not take sides for a long time. He allows the two most important women in his life to bite each other, play dirty tricks to one another, fight for power, prove themselves before each other—sometimes quite roughly. And this is the better scenario because some men never really cut the umbilical cord. If "Mommy's boy" creates a frontline in union with his mom against you, think very well whether you belong in that family or not, and whether he is the man you want to spend your life with.

Our mother-in-law most often attacks us with labels referring to our skills as a housewife. She usually sees us as "a poor cook", "lazy", or "grub and slattern". And she states it—openly, or in a roundabout way. According to her, we have never cooked anything tasty, our house is dirty and untidy, her son's shirt is not ironed, and his shoes are not polished, and finally—the table cloth has been hanging to one side for several days now. At first we agree with her because we were raised well, we even try to "mend" our ways, but often she fails to appreciate our efforts. Gradually, we start to pay less and less attention to her and respond sharply only when she goes too far. The labels she sticks, almost don't touch us until we hear them from our husband. And this happens sooner or later because she has managed to convince him behind our backs through her constant bickering and pointing a finger at our flaws. What shall we do? Kicking her out of the house is impossible, as her son will not allow such an extreme measure. To respond in the same manner won't do either, as it will inevitably lead to ugly scenes, from which nobody benefits. But it's equally difficult to keep silent.

***K. N. 36 years old**, made the extreme decision to leave her husband because of the constant criticism from her mother-in-law and the unbearable tension she created in the family. „She used to come to the house at any time—says K.N.—She would look around critically, she would check the furniture for dust, she would focus on a little speck on the table cloth and would start ranting—how my mother had failed to teach me anything, how I slept in all morning while the house was buried in dirt, how windows should be* *cleaned every week, and I haven't touched ours for months. She even started taking my husband's ironed shirts out from the closet and ironing them again (better than myself, of course). She would check them for missing buttons and would be very happy when she found one because that for her was yet another irrefutable proof that I was a grub and basically no good. One day, I couldn't take it any more, packed my suitcases and left for the farthest possible town. Soon after, my husband arrived and asked me to go back to him, but I refused. We got together again after two years, after she died, but I still hear the labels she poured over me that came through my husband. I try not to let them too deep inside, but it is not easy. I still have the feeling sometimes that she is standing between us."*

There are numerous such cases of psychological harassment of the young wife by her mother-in-law, but it is not necessary to resolve them by severing all contact. Sometimes we can neutralize the incipient conflict with milder means.

Her son—our husband can help a lot in calming the relationship with our mother-in-law. He can help us find the much needed compromise, without taking sides or pouring reproach in one direction or another.

Another hot spot appears in the daughter-in-law/mother-in-law relationship with the birth of a child in the family. You can guess the most frequent labels we receive from the loving Grandmothers—we become "bad mothers", "with the wrong pedagogical approach", "weak" because we are not strict enough with our punishments, or we spoil them too much. Naturally, we turn into even worse housewives, which we have no problem admitting, as the little person becomes the center of our attention. But if we get only nagging and remarks, without any help from her, we inevitably will become hostile to her. The good news is that the labels she gives us in this period do not stick much, as motherhood is the time when we feel strongest and least susceptible to external influence, especially when it comes to our children. Perhaps, it's an instinct, perhaps we really become stronger . . .

If you are already a mother-in-law yourself, it is possible that you have a different point of view. I even hear you say that "you can never please a daughter-in-law", that you do everything for her and still she is not happy, that she is headstrong and does not accept any advice, that she does not respect your opinion . . . Well, maybe it would be better that you didn't do anything for her unless she asked you to, and better stop giving her unwanted advice. Otherwise, she might interpret your good intentions to help her as interference as attempts to control her and you will wake her instinctive resistance. You don't want her to agree with you on everything, be polite on the surface while boiling with anger inside that she has acquired a mentor who watches her every move under a magnifying glass, do you? Can she give you labels? I don't think so. It seems with age we become less susceptible to new labels, and in the case of your daughter-in-law, your strongest protection is the fact that you feel so much better, knowledgeable and skilled than her in almost every respect. Maybe you really are . . .

Of course, there are many mothers-in-law who are only too happy to help the young family without imposing on them their way of life and their understanding of how the household should be maintained, and the kids raised. They remain outside the subject of the labels, though, so I'll spare my praise for them. I just wish you such a mother-in-law. If you already have her, ah well, you can skip this chapter.

OuR ChiLdReN

Believe it or not, at one point, our kids can label us too. As our age progresses and they grow up, the layers in our relationship with them shift. They become mature people, with their own belief systems and opinion on many issues, while our development gradually slows down. It is not necessary to be offended by them in order to feel rigid, backward, neglected, or have your reputation undermined. There is no drama in this, unless we create it. Not all of us do it—just the more sensitive among us and those who, due to poor health, are full of negative feelings and suspicion. If we take every insignificant remark, made by our children, as a scathing criticism, debasing our personality, it is time we started to think if we have not become too susceptible to new labels; whether we are not underestimating ourselves if we seek and find confirmation of our flaws in their words.

Maybe we have started to forget, maybe we do not pay much attention to how we look, or to our hygiene, maybe we have become less tactful and rather sharp, as opposed to what we were when we were younger, perhaps we have succumbed to vice which we controlled within socially acceptable limits before. Or maybe we criticize them too much which triggers the respective reaction in them to tell us in turn what they dislike in us?

It is hard to give advice to parents about their relationship with their grown up children. Every situation is strictly individual—there may be 30-40 year-old tension between the two parties, the emotional connection between them may have been broken, or it may simply be a matter of the most natural concern of children for their old parents, which the latter perceive as an attempt at control or belittlement.

Labeling ourselves

Sometimes we label ourselves and consolidate the labels through the years, but to some extent, these labels have been influenced by the repeated attitude and judgments of others towards us.

I used to have a girlfriend who desperately wanted to lose weight, regardless of the fact that everybody thought she was one of the slim, tall and very well built girls in the class. I don't know what had caused this yearning to be skinny, and there's no way I can ask her now as our paths parted a long time ago. It is quite possible that she isn't so slim anymore, but she might have forgotten her mania for "skin and bones". I hope so. I hope she has accepted herself and is happy with herself the way she is.

I also became an involuntary witness to a more drastic event.

Our boss's daughter dropped by at the office, and we all felt sorry for her as she was so thin and frail. She smiled shyly and said she was OK now, that she weighed a whopping 41 kg. She answered our puzzled looks with the simple "I nearly died last summer—I barely weighed 26 kg. They barely saved me." I did not get the underlying reason for her suicidal behaviour, I could not bring myself to asking more questions, so I contented myself with the vague explanation about overdoing a diet.

I still fail to understand . . . and science does not provide any explanation as to the reasons behind the voluntary starving to death.

Perhaps somebody told these girls that their figures left a lot to be desired, or even mentioned the loving "chubby", and they, in pursuit of perfection, undertook that attack against themselves.

At this point, I have to note that nobody is perfect. Nobody is equally good at everything, always there's something, somewhere that is not quite right. And if you accept this simple truth, you'll find it easier to define your priorities—in what area you should try to be unsurpassed and in what other area you should accept your mediocrity. It may not be easy, but do try.

Personally, I recently was stunned by the realization that I am an average, white, middle-aged woman. Yes, I am—if most of my friends, relatives and acquaintances do not see anything special about me, that is who I am. In my head, I have always been great—since earliest childhood up to this moment. But nobody perceives me that way. Why?

Because nobody can see me anymore under the pile of labels I carry—given both by others and by myself while trying to survive, to rise above them, or in coming to terms with the helplessness to develop my true potential.

I will try here to separate the labels I myself have given to me (noting, though that others have contributed to them as well). Some of them are objective, other are an expression of the way I perceive myself. The labels we can put in the "objective factors" column can relatively be accepted as neutral labels, they are a given, which cannot be changed, whether we like it or not. Just the way we cannot change the colour of our eyes or grow up by another twenty centimeters.

Approximately, my list looks as follows:

I am:

- *different, "offbeat",*
- *intolerant towards injustice,*
- *patient,*
- *suspicious,*
- *self-critical, a bit too much so,*
- *sometimes oversensitive,*
- *an average housewife (or rather I do not seek perfection in this area),*
- *monogamous, and I require the same from my partner,*
- *my skin is a bit darker than I wish,*
- *slightly slouching.*

I am not:

- *tall,*
- *slim,*
- *punctual. I am almost always late for my meetings.*

I have:

- *beautiful eyes,*
- *hair—not too thick, and it grows slowly,*
- *sense of humour,*
- *big bust.*
- *a mission.*

- *My independence is too important to me.*
- *In my partnerships (business and intimate)I do not need to dominate, but I cannot stand persons trying to dominate over me either.*
- *I don't lie and can't stand people lying to me.*
- *I am forgiving and do not clog my being with bad emotions and vengeful thoughts.*
- *I achieve everything I set out to do but slowly and with great effort.*

And this is my present list, the one from years ago simply should not see the light of day.

Did you manage to see me beneath my labels? Or you are asking yourself what is this quirk of Nature that can analyze herself until she turns blue? If you are not at least a bit inclined to do that, then this book is not for you. But if I have piqued your curiosity, please continue to read.

And now that you've established that I am a middle-aged woman, with an average size, far form the size of a fashion model, with a big bust which makes her slouch (since childhood—I'm pointing this out because back then it was not a cause of pride to me), temperamental, touchy, but otherwise reliable, as long as you do not lie to her and beat about the bush, sit down and start writing your list. Do it honestly, without holding anything back, put on that list even that fleeting thought that passes through your mind—it is still important.

Try to differentiate between your own labeling and the labels others attached to you. Assess them to find out which ones are acceptable to you and which are unbearable. And remember, the principle of elimination is from the recently received to the older ones, from the ones that were granted to you as a present by the people you encountered in your life, to the ones that you "produced" yourself.

Habits

Perhaps, you are asking yourself what habits have to do with labels? They have a lot to do.

Habit is that mechanism which spares us a lot of physical and mental efforts in exploring the world around us. Once we have learnt to do something in a certain way, we continue to do it exactly the same way for years. The emotional aspect of it is a bit different—we react in one and the same or similar way to the same or similar stimuli. Good, or bad, the habit signifies comfort and security. Its "maintenance" does not require efforts as opposed to changing (even the smallest) that we decide to make in life.

The labels we have been carrying around for years, be they good or bad, have become a part of our identity. It doesn't even cross our minds that we can change something within us, no matter the stage in our life. And yes, we can do it, but it is easier to say: "I am like that"; "I've always been that way". Isn't this the voice of habit which through the years has played the main supporting role in the consolidation of our labels?

Our minds are covered in labels, both positive and negative, given to us by others in the process of interaction or are self created. As noted in the beginning of this chapter, we are not going to review the positive ones as even though they may not be 100 percent true, they are helpful to us.

The negative ones are harmful, and if we haven't done anything to get rid of them for years, they have become a part of our "comfort zone", as psychologists call it. And this is exactly the habit which makes us react the same way to events, words and gestures. Believe it or not, physical pain and heartache can also turn into a "comfort zone".

Years ago, I came across a study on addiction to heartache. I cannot quote the author or the publisher, as I do not remember them, but I am inclined to accept the conclusions from the study, as I am intimately familiar with the condition.

The study maintained that when experiencing negative emotions, the brain releases certain biochemical substances. If the situation is repeated often for a long time, the brain gets addicted to them and wants its fix. Ache addict! How does it sound to you? And yes, they exist. I had been one of them for a long time. I don't want to remember that period of my life, but if I have to define it, I'd say this condition resembles a swamp in which you sink deeper and deeper. Self pity and suicidal thoughts every day, for weeks on end! You cry for hours, and after that you feel lighter . . . so you pick yourself up, do some laundry or cleaning, some cooking, and once you've got your fix, you are half way through to normality and can almost do your chores.

Crises are short at first and occur at relatively long intervals, then they become more frequent and sideline us for longer and longer periods of time, paralyzing our will to act.

This condition can continue for days, weeks or months until it turns out that the person cannot get out of it alone. At that point, no self-help books will be of any use to them as they need specialized help.

FailuRe

According to the NLP theory, every failure is viewed as a step towards success. But show me that person who is indifferent to failure.

There are those of us with faces of stone who can hide the hurricane of emotions in their hearts behind the mask. Others will even attempt self irony, turning everything into a joke, just to prevent us from seeing how much they are hurt, or are angry with themselves for failing to overcome an obstacle.

No human being finds failure acceptable. And while some get themselves together, gather their strength in preparation for the next challenge, others sink into self depreciating moods, blaming themselves, external circumstances and finally start labeling themselves. And as already mentioned, it is most difficult to remove the labels we give ourselves.

Have you seen the reaction of a kid, who after numerous unsuccessful attempts to solve a problem, finally gets it? He slaps himself on the forehead "Dumbass!", putting into the gesture and the word all the anger with his belated resourcefulness. We do the same after each failure, though we do not slap ourselves and there's no mention of the word "dumb". If someone else reproaches us as well, instead of offering some consolation, the situation becomes even worse.

Negative self-talk, no matter what words you use, results in insecurity and fear of the next challenge. You will not overcome it with fear and insecurity, though you may miss it, i.e. you may run away from it. You can run all your life, but bear in mind, it's unhealthy . . .

So, do not grind your failures for too long, analyze them for a couple of days, draw your conclusions and move on.

Do not let thoughts like:

> „Everything works against me."
> „I am not a lucky person."
> „Things don't come easy to me."
> „I am no good" and other such, get stuck in your mind, because gradually these statements will sink from your conscious mind into your subconscious mind; in other words, you will give yourself a label that is very hard to eliminate.

What can you do to avoid the next failure?—Something very simple—rehearse for your success. Visualize in detail how you pass in flying colour every stage of your next challenge. See yourself as winner and feel the emotion behind it again and again before you face the actual challenge. It doesn't matter whether it is a difficult conversation with your boss, an interview for a new job, or an important performance before an audience. When charged with a positive emotion, you will be able to give it your best, and your chances for success will multiply manifold.

Even if you fail, at least you won't have any reasons to blame yourself that you are a complex-ridden flop.

A good example of the impact failure has on our overall attitude, and the force of habit is Jorge Bucay's story "The Elephant in Chains" from his book "Let Me Tell You a Story". Here is an excerpt:

> **"The circus elephant does not escape because it has been attached to a stake just like this one since it was very, very small!**
>
> *I closed my eyes and imagined a defenseless baby elephant fastened to the stake. I am sure that in that moment, the little guy pushed and pulled and tired himself out trying to get himself free. And, regardless of his efforts, he couldn't do it because the stake was too strong for him.*
>
> *I imagined him tuckering himself out and falling asleep and the next day trying again, and the next day, and the next. Until one day, a terrible day in his history, the animal accepted its futility and resigned itself to its fate.*
>
> *That enormous powerful elephant that you see in the circus does not escape because, unfortunate thing, he thinks he can't.*
>
> *He has that memory etched into his mind: the futility that he felt shortly after he was born.*
>
> *And the worst part is that he has never returned to seriously question that memory.*

Never again did he return to test his own strength.".

The effect of the spotLight

Imagine yourself on stage, the spotlight is moving from one end to the other and from time to time, falls on you. How do you feel in the spotlight? It's a bit uncomfortable, isn't it? All eyes are on you, your tension grows, your fear of failure too.

In many situations in life we feel as if we are on stage, i.e. we exaggerate the significance of other people's reactions to us, when they say and do things without paying much attention how others take their words and behavior. They are on stage too, but in their own spotlight. Sometimes however, how they are perceived by others is more important to them too. This, in a nutshell, is the "effect of the spotlight", which sometimes creates serious problems for us. In what way it will affect us, depends entirely on our attitude towards ourselves. If we are too self conscious, we will think that everybody notices our flaws and our physical imperfections. If we are more confident, we will think that our qualities shine in the spotlight. While the truth may be, that in both cases, nobody pays any attention. Because the spotlight is in our heads, it shines its light on our idea of ourselves, and does not show what others see and think of us.

In any case, we are the center of our own attention and the "effect of the spotlight" occurs in each one of us in different degrees. For the person with the negative labels, the situation is a bit more complicated. Because after each contact with another person, they feel a bit apprehensive, as if something is not quite right. They ask themselves a thousand questions—did they present themselves in the appropriate light, what impression did they make, did they embarrass themselves, did other people like them, etc., etc.

---

* Tranlated by Michael Levin

EXERCISE
Dim down the light

I offer you an easy exercise which you may do at home first, and when you learn to do it well enough, you can apply it while communicating with various other people.

For the purpose, you must have a movable lamp and you should be able to adjust the light. The appliance is called "rheostat" and is available at stores selling electrical appliances. Stand in front of the mirror, point the lamp at yourself and turn the switch for maximum light. Have a good look at your reflection and pay attention to the things that you don't like in your face. Gradually dim down the light and continue to observe your image in the mirror. Pay attention to the sensations in your body—heat, prickling/stabbing pain, breathing, palpitations. Continue to dim the light, until the imperfections you noticed in the beginning become barely visible or disappear completely. The light is dim, the face in the mirror is still yours but without the details that bother you. If you haven't overdone it and completely turned off the light, you might like what you see. Pay attention to your sensations and remember them.

As you continue to practice the exercise with the lamp and the mirror, you will be able to visualize the image without the help of the lamp and the mirror, and call the same sensations fast and easily.

It is then, that you can go to the next stage—recall the image and sensations when you actually interact with others.

And you know what? There's no point losing sleep over our small imperfections, because other people pay little attention to the details of our appearance, our behaviour, our character, unless they are directly affected by it. As I previously said, they are in their own spotlight and with relation to them, we are somewhere out there, in the twilight.

Guilt

The feeling of guilt is very personal, it nests deep inside us, it burns us, eats us from the inside, makes us weak and vulnerable.

Both extremes—the one whereby no guilt or remorse is felt about anything, and the opposite—guilty all the time about something, are pathological. The majority of us occupy the middle ground. Most of us are not equally good in all areas of life. And we know it. The bad thing is that when someone else senses our weak spots, they start attacking us right there. Unfortunately, they are those closest to us, who have got to know us in the long cohabitation or close relationship.

Why do THEY attack us? Why is it them who make us feel guilty? Even if they don't realize that, they hurt us, their instinct to dominate guides them on a subconscious level. There is no living being which does not seek to dominate over its fellow beings. But that's why Man is Man, because he has other means of expression without having to resort to blind instinct.

Those who suppress us, harass us verbally or physically, manipulate us, making us feel guilty or inferior, are weak people—their arsenal of means to establish themselves, is quite poor, they have remained at a rather primitive level emotionally if they use aggression when communicating with others. Or perhaps they are complex ridden persons, who feel weak and insecure, and they need to offend and demean others in order to rise at least a little in their own eyes . . .

The other reason to be treated this way is us. Somehow, we have put ourselves in the weak position, allowed to be treated this way, and now we gather the bitter fruits of our previous (probably long-term) behaviour. As we cannot change them by pressing a button or with a magical wand, we'd better start changing ourselves. The change in our behaviour will cause a change in their treatment of us. It is not easy, but it is worth the effort. Have you heard of the "butterfly effect"*?

One small flutter of its wings here, in time can cause a huge change at the other end of the world. By making even the smallest change in ourselves, we too, imperceptibly change the world around us.

SusPicioN

Why are you suspicious and distrustful?

Seek "the roots of evil" in your earliest childhood and school years.

I don't know who wronged against me in my childhood years, but I remember being suspicious as a child. When I started "unpacking" from labels, I remembered the thousands small events that had hurt me. I had forgotten them a long time ago, but they had left me a legacy of mistrust and suspicion.

I also don't know where we went wrong with my younger daughter, but at one point she used to drive us crazy with her touchiness on all sorts of occasions. We called her "Miss Fret", at the mention of which she would slam the door and refuse to have dinner with us.

I don't know whether I managed to cure her completely from her suspiciousness, but I think I neutralized it by telling her about a colleague of mine whom we called "The Universal Conspiracy". Through a simple example, I showed her how she looked to the bystander, and how pointless it was to cry her eyes in her room for insults only she has heard in what we've said. To what extent I managed to handle her suspiciousness, only time will tell, but I am noticing her handling jokes better and better, and she even tries to master the art of self-irony.

---

* The name of the effect was given by Edward Lorentz in his work "Theory of Chaos" and is derived from the theoretical example of a hurricane formation, also known as "sensitive dependence on initial conditions" of some non-linear dynamic systems.

As to the colleague called by us "The Universal Conspiracy"—she was indeed unique. God forbid she overheard something and asked you to repeat it right this minute (for example, you have made a comment about your boss and right when she insists on telling her why you are laughing with your colleague, he passes by), she would raise hell, thinking that it was her we were mocking—it's unbelievable what monstrous offence suspiciousness can create.

She was capable of snarling at you if you asked her the time: "Now what? Are you mocking me? You think I don't have money to buy a watch?", while the monitor was right before her, and all she had to do was look down to the right corner and tell you the time.

Suspiciousness speaks of insecurity and rather underdeveloped (or completely missing) foundation of our confidence and self esteem. If it ever existed, it has probably eroded under the labels—given both by others and by us.

There's a lot to work on, but you will have to go back to your earliest childhood, or even before that (alone, or with the help of a specialist), in order to uncover the small events that had produced the labels, which today you probably do not recognize as such, but they, nevertheless, manifest in your suspiciousness which hampers your communication with others.

Mentioning "before your earliest childhood", I remembered that both my younger daughter and I have not been "planned", we came as a surprise to our parents, which confused them rather than pleased them. So, perhaps, our mutual trait "suspiciousness" is due to extent to the similar circumstances around our appearance into the physical world . . . or even the circumstances before we were born? (There are numerous studies on the fact that babies "hear and see" what is happening around them before they are born and they absorb the peace or tension which go with the mother's pregnancy.) Because neither my sister, nor my elder daughter has this inclination to read reproach directed at her into every word others utter.

They have been expected, as opposed to us, who just dropped into this world from the sky, throwing our relatives into confusion.

What I am telling you may sound like soul stripping but is actually an attempt to make you think of even the tiniest things that have, perhaps, helped you develop your suspiciousness and mistrust.

To find out how wrong it may be your idea of the opinion that others have of you, perhaps it would be a good idea to have some fun with the "Jars" exercise.

EXERCISE
Jars

The exercise is usually done in a group. It does not have to be a therapy group, you can even try it at a party, where not all of the guests have known each other for years.

In the first part of the exercise, the participants are offered to imagine that they are a jar of something, and they have to think what the label would be that best reflects other people's opinion of them. They also have to think what labels would suit the other participants best if they were jars.

In the second part of the exercise, the participants will have to think that they are inside the jar, and the rest of the world remains outside. They have to write down their thoughts, feelings and bodily sensations during their "stay" in the jar.

After both parts of the exercise are completed, a discussion should follow.

Note: *You'd better stop reading now and check your own perceptions in accordance with the above described method. The explanations below would "prompt" what you have to see and would spoil the spontaneity of your perceptions.*

The perceptions and sensations, caused by the exercise, vary to a great extent, but on the whole reflect the way we see ourselves through the eyes of others (in the first part) and how we feel when interacting with the outside world (in the second part).

In the first part of the exercise, the association with food is frequent because of our well established idea that jars usually contain food, but apart from the pickled chilies, pickled gherkins or raspberry jam, some of the participants see coins, nails and tacks, even chalk.

When they are "inside" the jar, some of the participants feel rather comfortable and protected, observing curiously what is going on outside; others find it narrow, suffocating, they feel they are being observed and are confused as to what they are expected to do. Some see themselves in closed jars, for others—the top is completely missing. Some see their jars neatly stacked on the shelves in the Mall, others are in a dark pantry. (The instructions do not state what the jar should be on purpose—open or closed, where exactly it is placed—so that the perceptions of the participants are not manipulated one way or another.)

(*Figure 3*)

The most interesting part comes when the sharing starts because it turns out that the labels others have given to each participant do not correspond at all to the ones the participant has given to himself. This happens too often in real life as well—we don't have a clear idea how others perceive us until they state it straightforwardly.

Tough Case

DiffeReNt ENViRoNMeNt

If by different environment we understand higher social strata, they too, label those who accidentally enter their circles, because they are conservative and elitarian, they tend to treat "Cinderellas" with contempt, even though they may not inferior in intelligence and education of the people of their usual circle.

I also came across by chance in such an environment—my work as a journalist met me with the love of my life—a famous person and politician who often led me to such secular parties.

If you haven't had similar experiences, let me tell you about mine—many of those born with a silver spoon and the so called "intellectual elite" are the greatest empty talkers and phrasemongers. Ill informed, they talk on global affairs, and global warming, discuss the classics in literature and music, yet they never read them or listened to them, they are fascinated by fashionable subjects, yet they don't know much about them. That makes them boring to listen to, boring to talk to! They put their whole hypocritical enthusiasm in telling their own, or overheard stories. But if you ask them a specific question, because you find the subject intriguing, they will look at you with contempt, leaving you without an answer, as they have nothing to say.

A person of more ordinary background, finds the company of such people a bit boring, but they have to nod in understanding, utter the respective interjections and exclamations at the right moment, smile and conceal their weariness with the company or subject. They are there out of love, friendship or business interest. And they do what is expected of them. At home, they can take a break from the 2-3 hours of hypocrisy.

But this environment, if the persons spends enough time in it, can label them "ignorant", "not brought up and educated well enough", "redneck" and what not.

The good news is that one finds oneself in this environment at a more mature age, when the person knows who she is, and thus the labels she might be given, do not stick long and can barely touch her.

Living with a man of higher social environment also is not easy. I will give myself as an example.

My husband often says "I don't know anyone who doesn't like opera", to which I usually reply (and it's true), "I don't know anybody who loves opera". Not long ago, I found out that he didn't know who Sting was. He probably doesn't know a whole lot of other things I know. I, on the other hand, don't know the things that have formed his preferences, not just the musical ones. Therefore, the argument is pointless—we have grown up in different environments, it is not possible to have the same values or have fun in a similar way. And there is no drama in this. It becomes a problem when he starts to exalt his esthetic preferences and diminish mine—thank Goodness, he rarely does that. And even when he mentions my "ignorance" in his favourite areas, he manages to get out of the argument with the words "I'm just surprised, it wasn't my intention to offend you." (See the chapter „Words are to be Blamed for Everything" and „Let's Stop the Telepathy Game")

When I first went to his place, I was so envious of his piano—probably because that was one of my childhood dreams that didn't come true. When I was little, the tiny apartment we occupied, could not hold such an instrument. Later on, when I had my own home, I could not afford it. He had it, the piano was part of his living standard. As it turned out, though, no one from his generation had played it, he even could not remember whether it was from his mother's family or his father's that he had inherited it.

I suppose there are many people who, for one reason or another, find themselves in an environment which is different from their usual. It's going to be difficult for them. If they are flexible, they will adapt. If they are not too sensitive, they will reject the labels which the new environment will try to give them.

I can't offer any advice in this case. I save myself through love. If he accepted me the way I am, what does it matter where we come from?!

We will have our arguments at home and, little by little, resolve our differences.

Immigrants find themselves in a similar, but a little bit more complicated situation. The clash between the two cultures may prove to be very painful for the newcomers. They may feel neglected, rejected, debased by the environment. This happens not because of their personal qualities as they usually accept the distance imposed on them, but because of biases, political convictions, and previous impressions from their fellow countrymen.

With a Sense of Mission

There are people who live with a sense of mission. Doesn't everyone?—you would ask. I don't know. I don't believe so, because I know many people who live day by day, come what may, never asking themselves "Who am I?", "Why am I here?", "What is most important in life?" If you ask them such a question, or share with them that you are seeking answers to these questions, at best they will tell you "You are too complicated" and the subject will be exhausted.

On the other hand, people, who live with a sense of mission, do not have it easy. They are more vulnerable because of the lack of understanding in others and are, by rule, hypersensitive. They become ingenious inventors, spiritual leaders, people with influence in society who are the driving force behind human progress, or total losers, ruthless criminals, suicide victims or people who spend the second half of their lives mostly in mental institutions.

These are the two extremes, but they are not the subject of this exposition.

There are a huge number of individuals in the middle, who manage to keep the balance—more and more at the expense of their confidence and self esteem, justifying their weakness in failing to fulfill their mission with other important things in life—kids, family, sick parents, career which no longer satisfies them, but they have become dependent on the income it brings.

Sometimes we don't have a clear idea of what our mission in life is, but we carry inside the vague awareness of it since childhood. We try one thing after another, sometimes we succeed, sometimes we fail, but our internal guiding system prompts us that we are not in the right place. So we continue to seek, sometimes to the end . . . .

Every fleeting thought like "What am I doing here?", "Is this what I wanted to achieve all along?", "Why am I not happy though I live better than most people?" is an indication of compromise made years ago with our true self, with our desires, strife, even with our talents.

We delay devoting to our mission even though we may know what it is with certainty. There is always something more important than this—to follow the impulse, to fulfill our most sacred desires. We think we have time, we think "Perhaps one day . . .", and the discontent within us grows.

Something similar transpires in the story of **V. L. 46 years old**, when she talks about her work and how she is unhappy with it.

Several years ago I was unemployed, and I couldn't find a job for a long time. At the same time, I was going crazy at home—I felt useless, although I did the housework with ease and my family was happy. Then it occurred to me that I could volunteer at some of the centers for women—victims of domestic violence. I thought I could be useful there. I didn't have any experience in helping other people in this situation, but it happened so that in my childhood, I had witnessed the physical harassment of several women from my nearest circle of relatives. And as an adult, I was a victim myself, thank Goodness, only of verbal abuse by my now ex-husband. I knew the problem. I knew that patience, resignation or hope that things were going to sort themselves out, were not a solution. Perhaps I could help, perhaps that was my mission in life, but guess what! Before my idea turned into a decision, I had found myself a job with quite a good salary and a position which suited me. As to the volunteer work—I postponed it.

For the time being, I cannot leave my job, my family needs the money. But I feel out of place there. Maybe one day, when I can afford it . . . I'll go help those women . . . or other abused people.

But let's go back to our subject—the labels, given to a person with a sense of mission.

They are misunderstood, their ego is hurt.

They are difficult to accept. Gradually, they become isolated. Not because they don't want to communicate with others, it is just that their subject of conversation does not present any interest to others and vice versa. If they manage to make friends anyway, they can count them on the fingers of one hand, and still there will be 2 or 3 fingers left.

At one point they get used to being misunderstood, yet every criticism, even the most benevolent one, hurts them.

If what I described so far is the childhood of a person with a mission, wait until their teenage years, when another problem would appear—interaction with the opposite sex.

Up to the age of 16-17-18, these people are haunted by labels, such as: "nobody understands me", „uninteresting", "unsociable", "ugly", "freak", "curmudgeon", and so, finding an intimate partner turns into a problem for them. I don't know how many of them change their sexual orientation, but I know of many women who chose to have kids without seeking husband. That was the biological part of their mission, which they fulfilled, and continued along their chosen path, guided by their inner sense of meaning and purpose in life.

I also know men with a sense of mission. They, too, are not cut out for marriage, but unlike women, they seek it. Why? Because while on their mission, they need help at home—support staff who would take care of their everyday needs—food, washing, ironing, cleaning and . . . sex from time to time. Poor support staff, unless they too have ambitions of their own, and do their chores among other things!

Labels in the form of offences and mockery affect mostly people who know what their mission is and are trying to follow it but face total lack of understanding in others. And because their mission is not a one-off thing, the results of which can be observed immediately, often in the eyes of others, the efforts of such a person seem meaningless, wrong and sometimes—completely insane. Such a person can easily be called "an oddity or freak", "dreamer", "naive", even a "liar" or "a madman". Would these labels have any impact on the person? It depends. It would hardly happen if they come from brief acquaintances who discuss him/her between themselves and call him/her with these, or similar names. But if the person hears these labels from the people closest to them, then they will surely hurt them.

I thought of offering an exercise, but the people with a sense of mission have heard so much uncalled for advice, inapplicable from their point of view, that they would better be left alone to follow their path and live their lives the way they see it.

ARe you going to fix the woRld?—oR how DoN Quixote tuRNs iNto a Sancho PaNza[*]

There are people with an acute sense of justice who cannot keep silent when their rights are violated or witness injustice done onto others, and they seek ways to prove they are right. They may have something different within themselves, or they were brought up that way. Perhaps, it was the environment in which they grew up—it doesn't matter. They

---

[*]   Don Quixote, fully titled ***The Ingenious Gentleman Don Quixote of La Mancha,*** is a novel by the Spanish author **Miguel de Cervantes Saavedra.** Published in the early 17th century, it is considered the most influential work of literature from the Spanish Golden Age and the entire Spanish literary canon, as well as a founding work of modern Western literature,.

Don Quixote and Sancho Panza are the two main protagonists who are diametrical opposites not just in appearance but as representatives of different social groups and character. Don Quixite is the absolute idealist whose head is in the clouds, while Sancho Panza is the embodiment of practicality whose feet are firmly planted on the ground.

are who they are—different, irreconcilable, fighters for causes. But, unfortunately, too often do they hear the cliché "Are you going to fix the world?" in reference to their reaction against injustice. These are valuable people who are appreciated too little. They usually show us how we all have to behave when our rights are violated, but we crush them with our resignation, with our indifference to such problems, by retreating into our peaceful lives, full of compromise. And we leave them alone. Often, we label them "conflict", we gradually isolate them, or they prefer the isolation themselves, after numerous attempts to be understood.

And if they don't become "smarter" with time, these people remain lonely in their fight for justice. As they fail to learn how to make compromises with the years, we promote them to the rank of "Don Quixote".

If there are such people in your circle, appreciate them, they are your tireless corrective, they are the ones who would always tell you the truth, no matter how painful, they are the ones that would lend you a helping hand when you are in a narrow spot, provided you don't ask them to go against their principles.

If you have been one of them for a long time, I think any advice is pointless. You will not change, and perhaps you are secretly proud of your nickname "Don Quixote"?! I.e. you like your label, and you carry it with pleasure.

But let's get back to the cliché "are you going to fix the world?" When you ask a child this question, or an immature young person, it is as if you are saying to them: "you are too weak to handle this problem." When you repeat it too often, or over a long period of time from your position as a parent, relative with an influence, or any other authority figure at some other level, this young person may believe you and really feel too weak to stand up for themselves; they may feel insecure, become passive, try (and maybe succeed) to sear their strife for justice and let themselves go with the flow. And why not? It's easier and . . . everybody does it. Standing up for your right to be different is a risky and lonely business, to be part of the mass gives a sense of security and peace. Fighting for causes, on the other hand, is exhausting and not always successful, while practicality, solving your own everyday problems bear fruit quickly.

The Sancho Panzas will readily invite the reformed (or maybe broken?!) Don Quixote at their table and will immerse him in a sticky mess of compromises, resignation and petty trickery. He will not be alone anymore but would that make him happy????...

Note:
The reason I wrote this chapter came from my elder daughter and her frustration during one of her first confrontations with the administration. She wanted to lodge a complaint, as she explained to me "not for myself, but because this is no way to treat people". I could not remember at the time where she could lodge her complaint, so I told her that it has always been that way, not to fret about trifles, just to let go, or something along those lines. This, however, further sparked her ambition and she declared that she would go through 10 administrations if needed, but someone has to put an end to this iniquity of office. I explained to her that in these 10 institutions she would face more of the heartless bureaucrats who do whatever they want with anyone who has turned to them for assistance. And after each argument of mine on the pointlessness of the endeavor, she repeated: "The situation is as it is because everybody keeps silent. Nothing is going to change this way. I will not leave things like this, no matter what the cost."

She went for a walk with her boyfriend, and I stayed home thinking. When did my little girl grow up so fast and now she is trying to fix the world? And while I was asking myself where she got this strife for justice, the inviolability of personal space, and playing by the rules from, I had already answered myself.

Why am I wondering now, wasn't I the same, have I grown too old, or I've simply forgotten?

In the sixth grade, who locked the door of the girls' locker rooms to the PE teacher who used to enter suddenly, without knocking? And then snapped at him that if he took me to the Principal's office, I'd just have the chance to explain why I had locked the door. Wasn't that me?

In the eighth grade who complained from the Physics teacher's "casual" but definitely lusty touches? Wasn't that me?

Who sued a famous businessman for discrimination? Wasn't that me?

Who got fired from a number of jobs because of their protest against poor working conditions (to put it mildly, because we are talking about an 8-hour-working day at 10-12° C, or cover up of corruption and other socially unacceptable facts—all in the name of the sponsor of the newspaper)? Wasn't that me?

Why am I wondering now? Wasn't I "a world fixer" myself? Even now, on certain occasions, I continue to be exactly that. My father was like that, and his father too, as far as I have heard, although I didn't get to know him well . . .

Maybe it's in our genes, but I'd rather say it's a matter of upbringing. Science has not yet given a definitive answer as to what the decisive factor is—the genes we inherit or the environment in which we grow up, and our characters are formed.

External Factors

„What would People say?"

This is not a question. This is a reproach which we often hear in our childhood and teen-age years. It is equal in power to "Shame on you!", "You are embarrassing yourself!", "This behaviour is unacceptable!" This is how we learn the norms of the society we live in, where everybody should feel comfortable. There's nothing wrong with that. Our parents raised us with similar phrases, and we, in turn, raise our kids with them. The worst comes later, when in our adult years we are capable of giving up our own decisions, our understanding of how life should be, in order to comply with "what people would say". But other people have their own problems and concerns and are hardly all that interested in what is happening in our lives. Well, sometimes they talk about us as we talk about those around us . . . but that's it. What they would say is of no consequence. Dubbing us this and that is for their own use and should not concern us one bit. Of course, there's always one concerned neighbour who would tell us what others are saying behind our backs, but the biggest mistake would be to accept other people's opinions of us as an authoritative truth and start doubting the correctness of our own decisions.

The minute we accept that their opinion is more important than ours, we surrender the control over our lives to them. If we start worrying about how we've been labeled, we gradually start believing them. We start living according to their rules, ignoring our own impulse and strife for a different way of life, for a different thinking. Their "must" and "must not" becomes more important than our "I want", "I think this is right", "I get kicks out of this", "I can't do this any longer", etc.

I know many women who have put off their divorce by 5-10 years, endured many indignities, dissatisfaction, physical and psychological harassment, justifying their masochistic patience with the mantra "What would people say?" Aren't we talking about those people, who heard the row but did not intervene because they thought it was none of their business? Think how many times you have interfered in a similar situation, unless, of course, the victim started screaming for help . . .

It is true that we care more about the opinion of our friends, colleagues, and the people from our social status. A stranger would hardly be able to offend us, and even if they do, the unpleasant feeling would not last long, i.e. the label won't stick. But we want people with whom we communicate on a daily basis to see us in a positive light. And to a certain extent we try to make them like us. This is natural, and there's nothing wrong with it if we do it effortlessly. If it starts bothering us, and we have to make compromises with our most sacred essence, with our values, with our interests, with our principles, maybe it's time to look for other companions, who will accept us as we are. We will sure feel much better in our own skins if we don't have to play roles, be careful what we are saying, and seek by all means to make others like us.

"What will people THINK?" is a more drastic version of this argument. Because if we accept that we can control people's thoughts (even with relation to what we are doing), then we got born on the wrong planet.

You have the leading role, you are the masters of your own life, others are part of the background. When you are passing by a building or a tree, do you get worried what they think about you? Or what they would say, how they are going to comment you in their own language? Maybe they don't like the colour combination of your clothes, perhaps they find your skirt a bit too short and your cleavage too deep, to say nothing of the colour and style of your hair . . . Well, accept people around you as part of the landscape and stop worrying about what they think.

Requirements and Expectations

Have you ever considered how many requirements you are supposed to meet in order to be accepted as a good, kind, hardworking, intelligent and generally—a positive person? Furthermore, you have requirements towards yourself which you seek to meet in order to feel complete, content, worthy . . . and generally a happy person. Thus, you feel pressure, both from the inside and outside. You are not alone in this. Often, balance evades us—we, somehow, fail to meet all requirement—both our own and other people's. We cannot be perfect in everything, least of all can we be perfect all the time. We say to ourselves "Next time I'll do better", "Next time I won't disappoint this person or that person"—there are always significant people whose approval we seek. As to our own requirements—we want to meet our own criteria in order to feel good—contented. Yet, too often do we find ourselves far from our ideal of perfection, so we find the situation rather oppressive. I will remind you again that nobody is perfect. People are generally good in one or more areas, while in other areas they are mediocre, or a total failure. Do yourself a favour, and do not allow your strife for perfection discourage you from making the important steps—publishing that book, sharing with the world that beautiful piece of music/poem you composed. Your work will always leave room for improvement, but sometimes it's the little imperfections in it that others might like and find attractive.

What happens when we constantly seek to meet other people's, or our own requirements?—It feels like constantly being examined. There's no day off, there's no vacation. We are in a constant state of stress. How long can this go on before we totally collapse? Not too long, for sure. And no wonder our mental state is unbalanced more and more often.

What is the way out?—One idea is to stop beating yourself up over small, or involuntary mistakes, over every imperfection in your work or relationships. We shouldn't be so hard on ourselves. As to the requirements of others to us—think them over, put them in a table under the columns "reasonable", "over the top", "unacceptable". Which are the unacceptable requirements for you? Trust your own instincts—they'll never mislead you. In the meantime, I'll give you a little hint: Unacceptable or over the top are all requirements which debase you, contradict your principles, convictions, and exceed many times your intellectual or physical abilities.

Expectations are directly related to requirements; we can even say that expectations are the milder form of requirements. It's as if they are saying: "I don't require anything from you, but I expect you to behave this way in this situation". They resemble requests, but they are not. They are still a requirement but manipulatively dressed. The choice is yours whether you would accept them, comply by them, or ignore and forget them.

Too often our expectations with regard to others fail to come true. Then, we are disappointed with the other person. We dub them "ungrateful", "insensitive", "inconsiderate", "heartless", "tactless" and all other adjectives with a negative connotation you can think of. And this is not an accident. Everything we tell them when we are disappointed (even if we only think it) means lack of a given quality in the other person, we EXPECTED that they had. The person may not have it, or he may be expressing it in a completely different way. Don't you think you are giving them a feeling of guilt? Isn't this labeling? Or do you think your words won't touch them because, according to you, they are "insensitive" anyway?

It will be very easy for you to find out how the other party feels if you remember a similar situation where someone else reproached you for their failed expectations. What was it like for you? Did you agree with the reprimand? Perhaps, a label stuck in your mind? Perhaps, it is exactly this label that in similar situations makes you expect similar reproach, even if your companion is trying to say something completely different? If your answer is "yes", then you have created other expectations, based on this label, or in other words—you have done another round of the vicious circle.

The easiest way out of misunderstandings, arising from requirements and expectations is a clear and specific conversation with the other party—without name-calling and voice raising, with more reason and less emotion . . . the bottom line is, the conversation should not turn into a scandal. If both parties honestly share their requirements and expectations of the other person, it will immediately become clear what is possible and what is not, where positions could be reconciled, and where they remain divided. Apart from being the more honest approach to the other party, instead of expecting them to have telepathic abilities and being angry when they fail to perform, this would be a relief to us as well—we would know what to expect, instead of playing the guessing game. And even if we don't like the way the other party is acting, we won't find fault in ourselves, i.e. their behaviour will lose the ability to label us.

To illustrate this, I will mention a few trivial expectation gaps:

1. The wife expects her husband to congratulate her on her birthday or their wedding anniversary, but he has forgotten. What follows is disappointment, injury, sometimes a row, because she interprets his act as neglect and underestimation of her own persona.

2. The man is coming back earlier from his business trip. Instead of being happy to see him, his wife is sulking—she's had other plans for the day. It does not necessarily have to be a date, as would be her husband's first thought when he feels her disappointment.

3. Parents, whose child studies in another town, expect him to call home every day. But that's the last thing on his mind. They suffer, they feel abandoned, neglected, on top of that, the uncertainty makes them uncomfortable. In their eyes, their son (or daughter) seems alienated to them and selfish person.

4. Someone did you a favour and expects something in return. The favour they are asking, though, is not within your power or violates your principles. You refuse . . . and are considered ungrateful.

D. S. 53 years old, *found himself in a similar situation when his wife's boss asked him to be her witness at her divorce. Until recently a friendly family, they were now fighting fiercely for custody over their child. At first D. S. agreed, but after hearing the instructions of the lady in question—namely, that he would have to maintain in court that her husband was an unbalanced drunkard and a gambler, who wasted huge amounts of money in the casinos of Las Vegas, he firmly refused to bear false witness. She even offered to pay his fare and a week's stay in Las Vegas to get him to know the environment, so that his story could sound plausible, but she could not get him to commit. His refusal deeply offended her, and she declared that the favour she had asked of him was completely legitimate, as she had helped his family at a difficult time by hiring his wife to work in hers company, and it was time they returned the favour.*

In all of the above listed cases, the party with expectations does not take into consideration the specific personality traits of the other party. Or it is not about not knowing the other party, but about a selfish desire for one's own expectations to be fulfilled. Well, real life does not always happen according to our wishes.

Instead of an exercise, I would offer you the Gestalt prayer by Fritz Perls—please, recall it often—personally, I get tremendous benefit out of it. Because it is not really necessary to wage war on other people's requirements and expectations, or to fight fiercely for ours, it is not necessary to feel hurt and label ourselves just because we are different people, with different feelings, thoughts and experiences.

Fritz Perls' Gestalt Prayer

I do my thing, and you do your thing.
I am not in this world to live up to your expectations,
And you are not in this world to live up to mine.
You are you, and I am I, and if by chance we find each other, it's beautiful.
If not, it can't be helped.

(Fritz Perls, 1969)

Note:
The subject directly relates to the feeling of guilt and suspiciousness which have been discussed in separate chapters.

Gossip

The gossip that we hear about ourselves can be completely fabricated, or it may be grounded in an intimate secret of ours which someone gave away—in most cases decorated with juicy details you never even dreamed of. Usually we get offended by it only in the second case, but sometimes we are not indifferent to the complete fabrications if they tarnish our good name. They, too, are labels—not in our minds but in other people's idea of us. They still hurt us, create problems in our communication and interaction with others, but cannot truly shake our self-esteem, should we choose to ignore them and forget about them as soon as possible.

Because it is unimportant who said what about us—it's all about our reaction to it. Should we choose to accept the judgment emotionally, we have already allowed it to turn into a label which would affect our future behaviour.

In this line of thoughts, it would be good to mention that gossip, through which we label each other, generally hurts our communication, as other people's labels have an impact on us as well. We are unaware of the fact that labels prevent us from getting closer to another person and getting to know them. We've heard stuff about them, they have a bad name, and so that rumour has reached us. And this prevents us from interacting in a normal fashion with this person, so we keep our distance, at least in the beginning, as if he is a leper. We are biased, and bias and prejudice are the enemy of all human relationships. Often our prejudices prevent us from getting to know the other person.

If it is someone close to us that "got a name", we suffer for them, even though the person himself may not care much about the labels.

AdveRtiseMeNts

Ads attack our self esteem and our fears; they feed our desire to be at our best, to be in tune with fashion, while actually they manipulate us and label us very successfully if we allow it. Few are the people who are immune to the advertising virus, and let's not forget—it attacks us 24/7, 365 days a year.

So, if you are still 30 and are anxiously staring at yourself in the mirror, looking for wrinkles, think again—is this your own fear, or your reaction to what you have seen on TV, on some billboard, or on the shop window of a store, selling cosmetics? Well, if your search is thorough, you will inevitably find one, and no matter how insignificant it may be, it would seem to you that the whole world is looking at it.

If you ask any dentist, he will tell you there is no snow-white enamel in nature. So if your teeth start to look discoloured to you and this "problem" bothers you almost every morning, think whether the reason is not the ad for that new toothpaste which "makes your teeth whiter in only a week."

You liked your curly hair until yesterday, and today it seems horrible to you when you look at the unrealistically thick, soft, glossy curls that float on the screen—and all this—thanks to the new hair balm with whatever . . . Not that we are not tempted from time to time to take advantage of these miracle products, only to find out that in most cases the result of their use is less than modest . . .

Hey, girls, don't think for a minute that my advice for you is to turn sloppy and unkempt—just the opposite. I only wanted to remind you that advertising and cosmetic industries earn billions from our complexes, small imperfections and our desire to stay young and beautiful forever. They declare they provide solutions to our problems but with their obsessive persistence they actually make them worse. That is, if we allow it. If we start observing ourselves under a magnifying glass, we will always find things we dislike in our appearance, and inevitably that will lead to labeling ourselves, for which even the most expensive, state-of-the-art cosmetics will not be able to provide a cure.

I don't even want to start on the subject of advertising drugs and food supplements. You can literally get sick if you give in to their hypnosis. The promise is that if you let yourself be under its spell and decide to improve the turnover of the pharmaceutical companies, "you will get cured" from all known diseases plus two or three yet undescribed ones as a bonus.

Live Marketing

The mention of food supplements made me remember a case when I was ignominiously thrown out of a meeting, only because I asked too many questions.

I saw this ad "Prospective business with minimum investment"—nothing is required of the applicants—no education, no special skills, no age, no gender, no nothing . . . Only to be communicative. The interview was set at a certain date and time, at a place which I could hardly find, but I got the vague impression that it was well guarded. With the very first shots on the screen, I understood that I was in the wrong place, but unlike the previous times, I could not get out unnoticed because there were only around 20 people in the small hall. The multi-level marketing company was familiar to me from previous attempts at "additional income"—I hadn't trusted them years ago, I didn't trust them then, but I had to put up with the acclamatory presentation. After that, one by one, live, came out people who had got rid of their health problems and tried to convince us what a miraculous product we were going to distribute, provided we signed some declaration. One of the speakers had shed unwanted extra kilos, another one had got rid of their anorexia, yet another one had reduced their blood pressure, somebody else increased it, one person had got rid of short sightedness, another of long sightedness . . . As you can guess—this is impossible. It inevitably raises suspicion and the normal human logic immediately registers the paradox. There's no such medicine that would be equally effective in both directions. It was clear that they were lying to us, nevertheless I was going to keep silent. The problem started when one of the presenters asked "Any questions?"

So I asked what the content of the panacea, that we were going to offer friends, relatives and strangers, was.

„The product is herbal, it contains over a hundred herbs in different proportions" was the answer.

„Anything more specific?" I asked again.

„Trade secret"

OK, I agreed, but since I had started anyway I could not but ask the most important question for me.

„Do we have to take it too before we start offering it?"

„*Is it moral to sell something in the qualities of which you are not personally convinced?*" *retorted the presenter.*

„*Yes—I agreed—you are right, but I don't need to use it.*"

„*Why?—he pressed on.—Don't you want to be completely healthy and have ideal weight?*"

„*I AM completely healthy and quite happy with my weight.*"

„*Then leave at once.*" *He snapped and my protests that I was asking logical questions, and he shouldn't throw me out were silenced by his shouting. Two muscular boys carefully pushed me towards the door and thus my career in the health and wellness business ended.*

My advice with regard to counteraction to the advertisement exposure is both simple and impossible—don't watch ads! Or at least ignore them, if possible. Follow your own style and needs. And doctors' prescriptions, of course.

Age Perceptions

There are many reasons why one feels old prematurely—exhaustion, health conditions, daily confrontations which drain our life force in no time.

The subject of this chapter, though, are the cases whereby other people or various everyday situations imply that we are old. To what extent we are going to succumb to the influence of the "environment" depends on our self-esteem, our own perception of the course of our life and last but not least—how sensitive we are to the age subject.

I don't know why but it is generally considered that women are more afraid of old age than men. There are no such statistics, or at least I don't know of any. This view is probably based on the fact that women are more prone to sharing their fears and concerns, and their attempts to hide a few years with cosmetics, fitness, plastic surgery (and often with a blatant lie) are far more numerous than the male attempts to hold on to youth.

Feeling old before you turn 30

Why a 25-30 years old person may feel old?

There may be many reasons, but the main ones are as follows:

—if a person's peers have already created families, the person risks to be labeled "spinster/old maid", or "(old) bachelor". Perhaps they think it's too early for them, perhaps, they are not ready to make the important step, perhaps they haven't met the right person yet, perhaps they have other plans for their life, perhaps . . . perhaps . . . there may be thousands of reasons which other people not only don't want to understand, but often don't see or don't perceive as legitimate.

Such persons often hear from parents, relatives and close friends remarks like: „Come on! What are you waiting for? Your classmates' children have grown up already, and you still don't dare tie the knot", „The Prince on a white horse exists only in fairy tales, no point waiting for him, get yourself together and do it", „Well, you are the only one who cannot find a man/a woman . . . why are you so picky?"

The fateful moment comes for most people, of course, but for the few for whom it does not, it is usually a matter of their own, conscious choice. But what should they do with the label people gave them through their uninvited compassion for failing to settle down, or with their biting remarks when they want to hurt them?

(Figure 4)

Jokes of the type "I'm still young, there's enough time" work for a time. Then they start feeling uncomfortable at parties—either because they are single among many couples, or because some "kind-hearted" person among their friends, playing a match-maker, has secured another single person from the opposite sex.

—If a person still has not chosen a profession, or hasn't got high enough up the professional ladder. The "high enough" is usually defined by the people around them—his mother, father, relatives, brief acquaintances and neighbours. Concerned, they ask "When are you going to make up your mind what you want out of life?", "When are you going to get back on your feet?" They provide advice—"It's time to get serious", "It's time to abandon youthful follies", and basically, they suggest that up to that moment this person has wasted his time, failed at his endeavours, he are incompetent, immature despite their advanced age. These labels in combination with the age reminder could oppress anybody.

—If a person already has a spouse but has no kids. Few people around could understand them if kids did not rank first among their priorities. They are reminded with, or without reason (especially women), that there's no time; that the clock is ticking. They often hear "What are you waiting for?", "You are going to miss the last train" especially from the people closest to them. Those who are not so close are by rule crueler, and label them "childless or barren" without much consideration that the person may have other reasons not to have propagated by now. The comparisons with the classmates whose children already go to school, or at least can say when they want to go to the bathroom, enter into circulation again.

Everyone has his own schedule for his life and no one else can make him to do something, if he does not decide to do it. If, under the influence of people's remarks, you start wondering whether you have missed any important events in your life, ask yourself whether you really want them, whether you need to do what is right by other people's standards. If you really want them, think what prevents you from making that step in their direction—there sure are concealed reasons, which you'd better be aware of, and probably—eliminate in order to make your wish come true. If, however, you feel inner resistance, this would be a clear indication that you have other plans and goals in life, and you don't have to abide by the council or insistence of others. Best tell them in plain text and ask them to stop pressuring you.

Old at 45-50

I already hear the comments of the 20-25 year-olds that a person at 50 is a goner and the labels "old bag", "uncle", "auntie", "geezer, relic, old fart", "walking obituary" (sometimes much more offensive) are completely justified by their standards.

From their point of view, youngsters are right, of course—their own parents are around that age, right? I. e. the 50-year old person is the previous generation which they, from the pedestal of their youth, often consider backward, lagging behind, rigid, and outdated.

But we are talking here of our own perception of age. Why would a 45-50 year-old person feel old, although they are in perfect health, full of energy, their libido is OK, and they have plans and ideas for the future? It happens more often than you think. A person may totally crumble down if their grown up child says: "Mom/Dad, you don't understand, times have changed, and you are still living in your ideas of 30 year ago". Similar feelings can be unlocked by the birth of a grandchild, especially if you are involved in the day-to-day care for it. It is true, every generation helps the next one, but if your grown up children offhandedly put you in the "Grandma/Grandpa" frame and decide that raising your grandchild is the only meaningful thing in your life from now on, take precautions.

Imagine you have another 50 years to live—it's not impossible, is it? Are you going to take care only of grandchildren from now on?

Your life belongs to you. What you do with it is your own business. Do not allow them to deprive you of part of it just because you are a Mom or a Dad. Don't even think of feeling old. Don't let others make you think that way about yourself either, as the label "old" may crush you in your most active age.

45-50 years is the age when a rather large number of people start their lives all over again—they change careers, get divorced or get married again, find the time and energy for a long forgotten hobby which was probably their calling anyway, but they had abandoned it in their youth for a number of reasons.

To the bystander these decisions may seem odd, and you may hear the following comments with relation to them:

- He abandoned his wife at 50 for a younger woman, given that they even have grandchildren . . .
- At 50, he decided that there was nothing more he could get out of chemistry, so he took up painting . . .
- From complete atheist he turned into a devout believer but some sect got hold of him . . .
- He saved up all his life, but when he hit 50, he got crazy and started wasting money away on parties and exotic destinations . . .

I am sure you are already thinking of the "mid-life crisis". And you are probably right. But I am sorry it doesn't come earlier:

- so that we can cast off, without guilt, any relationships that do not suit us, without thinking how this may affect our children and parents.
- so that we can swap the profession that earns a living with a profession that is a calling.
- so that we can be who we are, and not who we should be.

I wonder why it takes us 50 years to find out how we should not live? In no way does it mean that you've been wrong all your life, that you haven't achieved anything or have no reason to be proud. No! But if you make an honest assessment, perhaps you'll be surprised to find out that you have, to a large extent, neglected your own wishes and feeling for the sake of others, that you have lived by other people's rules (be it in the family, or within the social context), that more often than you wish to admit, you have not been yourself. If you think you can go on playing roles for another 50 years, go on and forget about this book. But if you are fed up putting yourself last, now is the time to start letting go of the prejudices, the manipulations, the limitations, imposed on you from outside, the piles of "musts" and "must nots", "should" and "should nots", "you are obliged to", "it's the right thing to do", etc.

You can start all over again in literally any area of your life where you feel discontent. New beginnings are hard. But they will prove even harder if you start by wearing your label "old". Eliminate it as soon as possible and look at your life with different eyes.

I made this change. If I can do it, you can do it too. From the many examples I gave you from my own experience, you have probably understood that I've had complexes and limitations, I've been covered with negative label all over—some—self inflicted, other—received as a "present" from my encounters with people; that in my attempts not to hurt others, I've hurt myself, but I finally managed to look at my life from a different perspective.

Things with my first husband had not been going well for years, but I was too patient. I was hoping that things would change for the better, and although the thought of leaving him occurred to me at least once a month, I kept on postponing my final decision. A very close relative of mine, barely reaching 50 (or perhaps she wasn't even 50 yet) died suddenly. She was 5 or 6 years my senior. And then, several days after her funeral, while I was making a salad for dinner, the following thought occurred to me: "What if I had only 5 years to live? Would I live them this way?" The decision to leave my husband came suddenly, unfortunately, on a sad occasion.

Two years later I endeavored to change my career as well—journalism gave me a lot, in return I gave all of myself to it too, but I have already gone too deep into psychology which has always been my hobby, and I devoted my time to writing books, which I've always known was my calling.

And several years later, my new love found me, just when I least expected it.

The decision to change my life came to me a bit late in life, therefore, I do not advise you to be endlessly patient. Problems do not solve themselves, and procrastination only makes them bigger.

Aging from Watching Too Much TV

Television makes us age. Don't you believe me?

Television is a powerful instrument for manipulation, through which pharmaceutical and cosmetic companies empty our pockets. But that's not enough for them—apart from our money, they want our confidence as well. First they take it through insinuations that we need their services, and then they return it to us against the money we are inclined to give them. Yes, I'm talking mostly of ads, but not only. Movies also instill complexes in us. One almost cannot see ordinary people there—all positive characters are young, beautiful and strong, no fillings in their glossy white teeth, not an ounce of excess fat on their perfect bodies—flawless.

Now, the negative characters are a different story—they can be older, a bit uglier (sometimes even sinister!), a bit chubbier, with thinning hair, they may miss a tooth, sometimes even an eye, or a finger . . .

So, whom do we want to look like? The fat and ugly ones? And if we fail to achieve perfection right away, how do we feel?

News anchors, who sometimes give us the bad news with a ridiculously irrelevant smile, also manipulate us in that direction.

It's true, most people don't pay much attention to the TV or big screen personalities these days, yet all that beauty and perfection flowing from the screen, affect us on the subconscious level. We start feeling older and uglier and farther from perfection than ever. Nobody is perfect, though. There are those who accept and love themselves the way they are, and there are others who are always unhappy about some tiny wrinkle, a white hair, or some little blemish somewhere on their body.

If you are touchy on the subject of age, try reconciling yourself to the idea that one stage of your life has passed, and a new one has begun. It does not necessarily mean that it's a bad stage—it's up to you how you are going to live it.

Think about it: When you climb a mountain, how long can you stay at the top? And what is more important—to stay at the top forever, frozen in your glory, or go safely down the slope and have the opportunity to conquer new heights?

If you allow somebody, or something to label you "old", forget about new heights, new pleasures (why not new love?), new friendships and challenges.

If you expect at this point some complicated methodological instructions on how to eliminate the label "old", don't. It's all very simple:

- do not let this label stick in your mind, just reject it the moment someone attacks you with it.
- Remember—biological age is for statistics and the administration. Numbers should not concern you.
- Avoid if you can funerals, christenings and weddings, i.e. events which remind you of the age.
- Avoid conversations about disease, do not read books and sites on the subject either.
- Do not allow yourself to sink too deep in trivia. Do something new or do something that you normally do automatically, in a new way (for example, brush your teeth, holding the toothbrush with the other hand, not the one that you usually use; choose a different route to work, change your dress style or the way you talk to the people in your usual circle). Even the small changes will switch off the automatic mode of your brain and new connections between the neurons will be created in time. The more new connections you create, the better your memory will become, and your creativity will improve.

Old age is a perception, not a measurable category. We either accept it and bog down in lament over the past, or refuse to acknowledge it and continue to develop and enjoy life. It is your choice.

Removal of Labels

Let's Fix the Crooked Mirror

Imagine looking at yourself in a crooked mirror. I don't think there's anybody, who hasn't visited such a popular attraction in their childhood.

How do you see yourself in it?—small, pointed head, short legs, as if cut in two, and your body—almost a square. Or your whole body has turned into a thin stick, about to break down. Or your nose has grown long like Pinocchio's, and your fingers have become a meter long . . .

Every crooked mirror deforms different parts of our bodies, and none of them reflect the reality of us. The same happens with our minds. We accumulate deformities/deflections throughout our lives because we cannot avoid interaction with other people. For good or bad, through their judgments they instill ideas about our own personality in our minds; in other words—they label us. Some people in our environment are well-meaning and honest, even when they criticize us; others are not quite so. But they are all mirrors in which we have looked at our reflections since early childhood. And none of these mirrors is perfectly straight, and none of them shows us the truth about us.

Well, it's time we "straightened up" the crooked mirror. Because the multitude of mirrors which have distorted our perception of ourselves through the years, have merged into one, to create our own crooked mirror, the reflection in which is far from likeable.

Imagine what your life would be like if the labels "ugly, stupid, clumsy, lazy, nagging, mediocre, etc." had not stuck in your mind. What if positive labels had stuck instead, such as "beautiful, smart, dexterous, energetic, tractable, talented, etc." What would your life be like in terms of profession, career, intimate and business partnerships, and friendships? Wouldn't it be different? Sure it would . . . but . . . whatever happened, happened.

Start changing today! And as I love to say, start straightening up the crooked mirror in which you see yourself and others see you.

You have to go many years back in time, but it's not impossible. Remember the situation, in which you felt fat, ugly, stupid, incompetent for the first time . . . and who told you that that's what you are . . . From what position did they judge you? And why did you believe them without question? Do those persons mean anything to you today, and you don't even know where they are, if they are dead or alive, or what they are up to? If they are no longer present in your life, why does their judgment of you continue to weigh on you? If you answer these and other questions, you will realize that other people's judgments and opinions of you should not burden and hurt you so much, neither should they leave a mark on your self esteem.

Do the following experiment:

Remember the important people in your life of 20 years ago. Remember also the feelings, related to them. If you kept a diary when you were younger, find it and read what you had thought and felt when interacting with them. Your feelings were shared by some of them, you had happy moments—your memory will also be charged with happy emotions. Others hurt you—you will feel the pain again, although not as potent as it was years ago.

Now, come back to the present and ask yourself "How many of those people who were important to you 20 years ago are still present in your life?"

I know the answer. I did this experiment—I went back to a town to which I had escaped from everybody 23 years ago, in order to think things over and make up my mind how to move on . . . or whether to move on at all. 23 years later, it turned out that out of the 10 people, with whom I had had a very strong connection, but also had conflicts and temporary misunderstandings, only 3 persons were still present in my life. Three of the others had died, I had parted with my boyfriend at the time, who later became the father of my children, and as to the rest—for years I had no idea where they were, how they were doing, and whether they were still alive.

All our encounters with others—be it for a brief moment in time, or more lastingly—are important to us, but in the end, each of us is in our own cobweb of relationships, we each develop ourselves and our own relationships with others and are responsible for the place we occupy in the human formicary.

Straightening the crooked mirror is actually the elimination of negative labels and their replacement with positive. The methods are not so numerous, and you are already familiar with some of them. Still, the bottom line is:

- rewrite your life story, starting from your childhood. Use NLP-method to change your memories. First, you describe the event as it happened. Then you change it the way you wish it had happened. You can keep changing the story until you find the most favourable version and start copying it until you manage to delete the real event from your memory and replace it with the fabricated one, which makes you feel better.
- dethrone some of your authority figures—you have long surpassed some of them anyway—in talent and skills you've required—you just have to believe it and trust yourself.
- Use physical ritual that seems appropriate to you to get rid of all of the oppressive labels.
- If you do sports, activate your thought during this activity: jogging—visualize how the labels fail to catch up with you; boxing—you beat them into a pulp; wrestling—you are the winner; paragliding—you are high above them, and they cannot get to you; soccer—that you kick them out; swimming—visualize the releasing of the negative labels as murky water which remains outside the area of your movement—with every stroke you make, you leave the dark water farther and farther behind you—ahead of you and around your body—clear blue waters.
- If you like dancing—visualize yourself dancing in a minefield of labels, which you manage to avoid, etc.
- and remember once and for all—you and you alone, are responsible for your own life—people come and go, therefore, their opinions and judgments should not affect your self-esteem so much.

- Remember your success, not your failures. Think of your qualities, rather than your flaws.
- Take care of yourself first, and then of everybody else—your energy is not endless—if you pour yourself out without residue and fail to take care of yourself, at a certain point you will collapse.
- Forget the word "must"—it puts pressure on us which we subconsciously resist both when we repeat it to ourselves or someone on the outside is trying to make us do something. Improve your motivation by using more pleasant words and phrases, like "I choose to do" or "I want to".

I am afraid many of us, busy in our daily lives and beset by many problems, seek in books like this one, fast and easy fixes to our problems. I must disappoint you (as I have been disappointed myself so many times)—there are no fast and easy fixes to your problems. We need to work on ourselves. Every day. You don't have time? Then think again whether you find time at all for yourself, your health, your appearance, your hobby. Perhaps you live "in service to others", making sure that you satisfy even their smallest need? What do they do for you? Do they do anything at all, or are they used to being taken care of . . . by you?

When you make up your mind to take care of yourself and your own peace of mind, they won't like it . . . But the effort is worth it—both for your and for their sake. If you stop being their "crutch", perhaps they'll learn how to take care of themselves?!—and this would be a priceless experience for them. If you start taking better care of yourself, you will feel important to yourself, the focus of your attention will change—you will discover what a unique person you are, and maybe you'll discover qualities in yourself that you never dreamed you had, which, nevertheless, deserve respect, trust and recognition.

We do, indeed, live in dynamic times. In the hectic pace of everyday life, we find time for many things, but not for ourselves—a familiar story. That is why I want to tell you a story of how I tried "to work on myself" among other things.

I remember I nearly got into a conflict situation, trying to do a simple exercise, recommended by Norbekov*. It's really uncomplicated—as you are sitting in your chair, you straighten up you back as well as you can, and you put a big smile on your face—this is supposed to cause a positive change in your body. Well, I practiced it in the morning, while on the tram, on my way to work, as I couldn't find any other time. So far, so good, but there was this one time, when obviously a complex-ridden lady sat in the seat across from me. When she saw the big smile on my face, she started throwing those nasty looks at me, fidgeting in her seat and in the end literally erupted: "What are you laughing at? What is wrong with me? Do you think you are very pretty?", and so on, and so forth. I got off at the first stop while she continued her angry ranting. How could I explain to her that it was Norbekov's fault that I had this stupid smile on my face that I wasn't laughing at her, but I was trying to cure my body and soul on the tram? I don't think she would have understood.

Therefore, my advice to you is to find a quiet place, where you will be undisturbed—it would be easier for you to concentrate, and you will not cause bewilderment and unnecessary questions.

It is important that you looked at yourself from a different perspective. This will not happen unless you make time for the recommended exercises and self-analysis (written or mental), in order to become aware of the repeated mistakes in your communication with others through your oldest memories.

How to Stop Being a Victim

What are the similarities and differences between being a victim and feeling like a victim?

---

*   Mirzakarim Norbekov is an alternative medicine master well known in the countries of the former Soviet Union. He is originally from Uzbekistan. He has written a number of best-selling books that explain his philosophy of feeling happy and living a healthy lifestyle, as well as his belief that patients should take an active role in curing their illnesses.

Let's imagine two situations which will help us realize that our experiences not always correspond to the actual circumstances.

Situation One

Imagine that you are in prison, sentenced for a crime, or kidnapped by bad people and kept for days and weeks in isolation, locked, chained, abused. You obey your kidnappers, you try not to irritate them, you do whatever it takes to survive. At the same time you are thinking to yourself: "If only I can get away, I'll do this and that and the other". And you'll probably use the least distraction of your torturers to try and escape.

Situation Two

In your workplace you feel unappreciated or out of place, but you do not leave. You are thinking—if you find another job, where colleagues and bosses are friendly, you would feel happier, yet you do nothing to find this "new job". Furthermore, you are insulted, underestimated, even abused at home—you want to leave home too, but you don't find strenghts in you to do it—you don't see a way out and the uncertainty scares you. And yet again, you settle for it. Why? Why do you think you cannot do anything?

Suffering is great in both cases, but what prevents us in the second case from breaking free and doing something for ourselves? It's the victim consciousness. We are so much into this role that we have started to believe that we are helpless against circumstances, that we are doomed to suffering and failure, that "it was written in the stars", and ultimately—that's our fate.

Being a victim and feeling victimized are two different things. You don't necessarily have to be abused or to have been subjected to criminal actions in order to develop the victim consciousness, although such an incident may have had a serious impact on your self-esteem. If you often use phrases like "I've no luck", "Things don't come easy to me", "Why me, always me?!" (for bad circumstances and events) and other similar phrases, then you have developed, or are developing a victim consciousness. Because you are attributing greater importance to external factors and people, rather than to your own efforts to succeed in a given endeavor. And other people and circumstances are constantly in your way, as if trying purposefully to prevent you from realizing what you have set out to do.

The labels you have received up to that moment, or the ones you have given yourself, are to some extent both a reason and a consequence in the process of developing your victim consciousness. The main solution for you, in order to get out of the role of a victim, is to learn to take responsibility for each one of your actions, and thoughts. This means that you should stop justifying your failures with other people's actions or circumstances.

Example One:

If you have been dubbed "irresolute", ask yourself what is it that you fear every time you have to undertake an action. Making a mistake?—Is that so frightening? We all make mistakes—there's no way we can learn unless we make mistakes (how would a baby learn to walk if he/she gives up after the first or second fall?) What would people say if you fail?—Really, is that so important to you? (For more detail see chapter "Failures" and chapter "What would people say?") Perhaps you feel more comfortable in the role of a victim? Because how would you otherwise complain of your unhappiness and bad luck, how would you attract attention and compassion of people around you? Psychologists call this "Secondary Benefits" from the role of a victim while their clients deny having such "ulterior motives". And they are telling the truth as they are unaware of the fact that the role of the victim brings them such "dividends". Although things happen at the subconscious level, the model of behaviour will have to be deconstructed by conscious efforts.

Example Two:

You don't like your profession very much and, naturally, you do your job at some mediocre level. You know that your colleagues consider you "mediocre, incompetent, with no prospects". On the whole, you have accepted these labels, even without being told in plain text, because you feel out of place in this profession. Think about it—why did you chose it? Or did someone else choose it for you? Perhaps your parents, because it's prestigious? Or you chose it yourself because 20 years ago it was trendy? Or it was because most of your friends are enrolled in this specialty and this made that choice easy? Whatever the answer is, it is obvious that you have left the responsibility for the choice of your profession in the hands of other people and to external circumstances. Today, you find yourself in the role of a victim due to the wrong choice of profession. But the choice wasn't yours. Why are you surprised then that it doesn't meet your needs and maybe your skills? And why are you still occupying this position if it doesn't satisfy you? Probably for the reasons listed above . . .

Example Three:

You are again in the role of a victim, only this time—of an unhappy marriage. Why are you still there, enduring insults, coldness and dissatisfaction? Perhaps you depend on your partner financially or emotionally? Maybe you are afraid to leave because you are not sure how you are going to cope on your own, if at all? Is this your belief, or have you heard too often from your partner "you are no good", "what can you do without me?" I know it's not easy for you—the labels from your life together haunt you, no matter how hard you try to get away, but they'll continue to haunt you until you decide to make an effort and get rid of them.

Perhaps you are not leaving so that you don't hurt your children or parents?—Don't worry about them, they are already hurting—especially the children—because they hear and see everything, they sense when things between Mom and Dad are not going well.

So, here you are—in the marriage-prison, you have resigned to the role of a victim and you undertake nothing. How long will it go on? Yours may turn out to be "a life sentence" . . . Don't you at least make escape plans? Even if you do, you procrastinate—you are waiting for the right moment. And when is the right moment?—When the kids grow up, and your parents pass on, so that you cannot hurt anybody with your divorce?

In the three cases, as well as in numerous others, getting out of the role of a victim goes through:

- Eliminating labels or at least diminishing their power;
- Accepting failure as part of life. Each failure teaches us something, and in this respect it's a step forward towards success;
- Stop blaming yourself for past errors as they were your choice at that time, in that situation, and nobody makes mistakes on purpose, right?
- Learning to take responsibility for your every action and thought. It's your life, you are responsible for what is happening in it, and everybody else plays a secondary role;
- learning to say "NO" when you don't want to fulfill a request, without worrying that you will offend the person making it. You can say "NO" in any situation if your intuition prompts you to. This is your inviolable choice, and nobody has the right to judge you for it;
- Looking at you life from a different perspective. There are good things in it for sure—focus on them. Thoughts are energy—as you attract pain into your life, so can you attract joy. The choice is yours alone, and so are the outcomes.

Let's Cure Addiction to Approval

We interact with others throughout our lives—from birth to death. And we cannot be completely indifferent to how they perceive us, what our relationship is with them. But when we are too compliant with their opinions, beliefs and positions, we lose ourselves, we are left with no mental energy to develop our own personality. Yes, we all want to be admired, but for some of us, the price is too high.

It is my firm conviction that the reason for the numerous labels we carry, which make us feel weak, vulnerable, dependent, and indecisive, is our desire to be approved, which in some of us has turned into addiction.

When we are addicted to approval, we often know better how others perceive us (or at least that part of ourselves we have tried to show them), than what is happening within us—with our thoughts, feelings and wishes. The focus of our attention is outside of us, or if it is not all that shifted, duplicity occurs in our perception of ourselves. It shows in our actions as well. We do, on a daily basis, what is expected of us, not what we want, thus winning the approval of others. And we become easy prey to manipulators; forgetting the magnificent word "NO", we are always available, agree to everything and really start living a life in service to others.

Addiction to approval is closely related to the fear of rejection, whose roots are somewhere back in childhood. Probably they told you "I won't love you any more if you continue to do this", or "I'll give you to the Big Bad Wolf if you don't listen to me", or "I'll take Mike to be my son because he is good, and you only make me angry". These remarks are uttered automatically when we are desperate to get our kids to obey us. It is amazing how very few of us realize that they leave deep marks in the child's mind, they instill in them fear of abandonment, and the feeling of helplessness in the little person is incomparable with any other feeling at any other stage in their life.

If you decide to overcome your addiction to approval, you will first have to accept that not everybody will like you, approve of you, and accept you. It would be healthier if you liked, approved and accepted yourself.

Because when criteria, with which we measure our personality, come from the outside, we will constantly seek to meet the requirements and expectations of people around us, we may never be ourselves. And this is so exhausting and unnecessary at the same time.

When you start making the change, some people around you may not like it. Because they will sense that they are loosing control over you, they will feel belittled, they may even start attacking you with new labels, manipulations and attempts to give you a feeling of guilt. Your true friends and close relatives, on the other hand, will be happy for you. I am sure they will support you in your strife to be in a more independent and self-respectful position in your relationship with the world around you. You will start liking yourself better with every step you make towards the change.

Words are to be Blamed for Everything

Words are the basis for communication with others. They are the intermediaries between our inner world and the outside world, which in turn, consists of a multitude of other people's inner worlds. Through words, we express thoughts and feelings towards other people and events. Therefore, we seek to find the right words in order to be understood correctly by others. But do all words (taken separately) have the same meaning for all of us? We hope so—at least for the community speaking the same language, but we are wrong. It is true, the differences come from the nuances we attach to the meaning of a given word, but think about how often it is exactly the subtle nuances that are the reason for our hampered communication.

The nuances in our feelings are transmitted not only through words, but through the tone of voice, body language, gestures . . . and frankly, sometimes, it's a mess. You tell me something, I understand something else, I am offended, you are puzzled, wondering what was so offensive or wrong in what you just said, and in the end—we both feel a bit ignorant.

If we fail to clarify things that very minute and bridge the gap between what was meant and what was understood, there's a chance that we label each other. Depending on the self esteem of each one of the actors, the following situations may arise:

- I may feel underestimated in a given area, and therefore, offended;
- you—misunderstood yet again and even a victim of manipulation, because you sincerely believe that I distort the meaning of your words;
- we are both convinced that we speak different languages.

N.M. is middle-aged, happily married and has a grown up kid. Here's what she shared in the Gestalt Therapy Group:

Soon after we got married, my husband told me one day: "My mother is somewhat angry with you" I was totally bewildered and told him with absolute certainty that he was wrong because his mother greeted me, smiled politely, etc. He continued: "Yes, but she doesn't talk to you." "So what—I said a bit surprised—she may not feel like talking, she may be tired". Then my husband explained to me that in his family, when someone got offended by somebody else, they simply stopped talking to them. If he hadn't told me, I would never have guessed. Because, in my family, in similar situations, we have always had animated arguments, we have even fought, but nobody would retreat before we clarified our positions.

This example shows that not only words, but the manner of communication also matters in how well we understand each other. And to a large extent, it is determined by our social and family background.

The "lost in translation" problem mostly occurs in communication between couples. The different ways men and women communicate also contribute to that. Men usually catch the essence of what is being said, completely ignoring the details. While we, women, are dying to tell our stories in detail, interjecting and interposing own comments on the story we are telling. And then we are angry with them for stopping to listen to us from one point on . . . I remember the comment of a colleague on this subject: "a man needs to be talked to in very simple sentences: subject, verb, complement. Once you start filling him in on the details and using complex sentences, he "switches off". I don't know if she spoke from personal experience, or she had reached this conclusion thanks to her work with clients, it doesn't matter—take her up on that advice—it's good. And then send me an e-mail and tell me if it works.

Let's Stop the Telepathy Game

Why do people think that they can unravel the thoughts and feelings of others? Telepathy is not a mass phenomenon. But as far as people know themselves, they are inclined to accept that one and the same (or very similar) thoughts and emotions cause the same (or very similar) behaviour both with them and with other individuals. This is a fallacy.

One of the reasons to consider that all of us feel and think in the same, or similar way, is relatively put, the same matter from which our bodies and brains are made. We are wrong again. The large number of gene combinations reduces to a minimum the possibility of two physically completely identical individuals. And even if such a coincidence occurs, they'll be identical only at birth, and from that moment on, with every passing day, they will start to differ more and more under the influence of the environment, in which they are growing up and developing their personality traits. I.e. we cannot expect that their brains would develop in the same way and that their mental states will overlap completely.

We cannot be sure that other people experience the world the way we do. When someone tells us: "I know what you are thinking", or "I know how you are feeling"—whether he really knows? How could they, if they are not in your head, nor are they in your body? They probably imagine, they put themselves "in our boots", but their emotions and thoughts could hardly be the same as ours, provided that every individual has different life experiences, different convictions and beliefs, and generally—a different view of the world. And it is exactly this approach to the world of the other which causes a number of misunderstandings in our communication.

Take me, for example—when somebody tells me "I know what you are thinking", or "I know what you are going to say"—it drives me crazy. Not just because of the confidence of the other person, but also because to me, it feels like an intrusion on my personal thinking space. Am I so transparent and predictable that you know what's going on in my head? Are you God? Not to mention that in less than 10 percent of the cases, those who challenge me this way, present themselves as telepaths. It probably happened to you too. This is a frequently encountered mistake in our thinking of the other person's world, although we don't always state plainly "I know what you are thinking".

Why do I dwell on this phenomenon in so much detail? Because it plays an enormous role in the creation of labels, in their instilment in our overall perception of ourselves, in the destruction of our confidence, in our interaction with others.

We often "hear" in other people's comments what is already on our minds, although their intention was to say something completely different. Just as frequently, our comments undergo similar distortion in the minds of other people. And it's not always suspicion, it's just that our brain makes things easier for us—it places what we've just heard next to something else we've known for years, at the slightest similarity between the two. If we are suspicious too, the emotional reaction to such a "hearing" can be destructive.

Let's review a few situations.

When we praise a child that he is a terrific mathematician, they are not always glad, because they think we underestimate their other qualities. At the age of ten, they don't know that Mathematics is the most difficult sphere of knowledge for many people, and highlighting this ability of theirs equals being praised for high intelligence in general.

A wife comes home and begins to tell her husband about her day: "Today, as I walked round the shops . . .", without waiting for her to finish, he interrupts her: "And how much money did you spend?" She mumbles "Money is all you think about", and leaves the room offended because all she really wanted to tell him was that she met an old friend she hadn't seen for years.

Someone begins to tell a joke to his friends, and always there's someone in the group who interrupts: "I know this one", because if you've noticed, many of the jokes start the same way. Of course, it turns out that the joke is completely different from what Mr. Know-all had in mind, but this does not prevent some people from continuing to think that they know what the other person would tell them after the first few words.

They had had only a few dates, when the man said to his girlfriend "you are very beautiful today". She accepted the compliment with a bit of controversy—on one hand—she was happy that he noticed her efforts to look well, on the other—she was thinking: "He doesn't find me beautiful enough in general if I'm beautiful "today" ". . . And all he wanted was to be attentive and tell her something pleasant.

Let's start Living HERE and NOW

Painful memories from the past and fear of the future can be detrimental to us. They numb our will to act, prevent us from making decisions, and pull us into the vicious circle of our thoughts of how we are incapable of succeeding, of having healthy and satisfying relationships, of being happy. Labels, "stuck" on our confidence and self-esteem at different stages of our lives, play a significant role in this. They trigger "preventive" thoughts, they pull us into opposite directions—back into our traumatized past, or into the anxiety-causing future. They never allow us to live fully in the present, which is the only time that we have for action, for doing, for building our lives, and essentially—for truly living.

For example, what do the following thoughts, to which you are probably susceptible, do for you?

> „I won't make it again"
> „I'll fail the exam"
> „All men/women are the same"
> „They'll fool me again, just like the last time"
> „I'm not a lucky person"
> „Everybody hates me"
> „Nobody understands me"
> „My life is a complete failure"
> „What if I make a mistake?"

They are not very helpful, are they? But then, you cannot escape them when you are about to make a step forward, towards something that you want in some area of your life. These recurring thoughts are an illustration of the strong connection between the traumas of the past and fears for the future.

You can guess which labels make you think that way. They cannot be removed with a magic wand, but when you start eliminating them, try to modify your thoughts in the following way:

„This time, I will probably succeed"
„Perhaps I will pass my exam"
„Perhaps there are good men/women"
„Maybe this time they will play fair"
„I am sometimes lucky"
„There are people who hate me"
„Some people understand me"
„There are successes as well in my life"
„There's little probability for error"

Repeat the transformed phrases long enough, until they start to sound natural to you.

You will notice that the power of the labels diminishes, and your "preventive" thoughts visit you less and less frequently. It will be much easier now to start with the positive affirmations:

„I will make it"
„I will pass my exam"
„There are good men/women"
„The deal I am about to conclude is fair and legal"
„I am lucky"
„Many people love me"
„Many people understand me"
„There's a lot of success in my life"
„I will do the right thing"

By repeating these affirmations, you will feel more confident than with the first group. You can increase their effect if you write them down every morning or if you record them and play them to yourself several times a day. The "state-of-the-art" elimination of labels and releasing of fears is the removal of the future tense from your affirmations—start thinking of the things that you wish to happen to you in the present tense, as if they are happening to you now.

EXERCISE
Encounter with yourself

Meet yourself of 20 years ago and yourself in 20 years. Remember what you were like 20 years ago and imagine what you would be like in 20 years. Talk to "the child" and the "old man/woman", give them advice from your present vantage point, from the state of mind you are in today, from your present experience and understanding of things. "Listen" to what they have to tell you.

A frequently used method in Gestalt therapy is the one with the "empty chair"—you have to put your past or your future "SELF" in it, to see it, to feel it, and to have your intimate conversation with it.

It is possible that you dislike both your past and your future image. But while you cannot change the past, the future is in your own hands—you create it today, although you are not always aware of that. You can neutralize the influence of the past through a number of exercises, but you cannot change it or delete it completely. So, you'd better not dwell on it for too long.

But you can definitely change your future by building up your "today" the way you want it—happier, more confident, more respectful of itself and more independent from the judgments of others and from circumstances.

Do not succumb to negative thoughts that it's too late to change and that you have missed all your chances. It's never too late to change, if you really want it.

Our past and future are connected through our PRESENT—the only time when we can do something for ourselves—improve our relationships, start working to achieve our goals and dreams, enjoy life, regardless of our past experiences and what is yet to come.

Because while we are waiting for the right time and circumstances in order to take the decisive step towards the fulfillment of our dreams, finding the right person, or our calling, the things that make us happy, the change which will help us feel good in our own skin . . . life may pass by.

The right time and circumstances may not come, we have to create them. TODAY!!!

So . . . start living HERE and NOW!

If you don't like something in yourself, or in your life, change it. It's never too late for that. Start today, do not procrastinate! Procrastination does not solve problems, it just sucks your energy out—the energy which you could use to make your life fuller and happier.

Perhaps you like everything in yourself and your life? Then how did you get to the last page of this book???